TOP 10

FLORENCE & TUSCANY

REID BRAMBLETT

EYEWIT

D1042972

Left **Ponte Vecchio, Florence** Right **San Gimignano**

LONDON, NEW YORK,
MELBOURNE, MUNICH AND DELHI
www.dk.com

Produced by Blue Island Publishing, London

Reproduced by Colourscan, Singapore
Printed and bound in China by Leo Paper Products Ltd

First American Edition, 2002
09 10 11 10 9 8 7 6 5 4 3 2 1

Published in the United States by DK Publishing,
375 Hudson Street, New York, New York 10014

**Copyright 2002, 2009 © Dorling Kindersley
Limited, London**

Reprinted with revisions 2003, 2005, 2007, 2009

Published in Great Britain by Dorling Kindersley
Limited.

A catalog record for this book is available from the
Library of Congress.

ISSN: 1479-344X
ISBN: 978-07566-4098-9

Within each Top 10 list in this book, no hierarchy of
quality or popularity is implied. All 10 are, in the
editor's opinion, of roughly equal merit.

Floors are referred to throughout in accordance
with Italian usage; ie the "first floor" is the floor
above ground level.

We're trying to be cleaner and greener:

- we recycle waste and switch things off
- we use paper from responsibly managed
  forests whenever possible
- we ask our printers to actively reduce
  water and energy consumption
- we check out our suppliers' working
  conditions – they never use child labour

Find out more about our values and
best practices at www.dk.com

Contents
Florence & Tuscany's Top 10

The information in this DK Eyewitness Top 10 Travel Guide is checked regularly.
Every effort has been made to ensure that this book is as up-to-date as possible at the time of
going to press. Some details, however, such as telephone numbers, opening hours, prices,
gallery hanging arrangements and travel information are liable to change. The publishers
cannot accept responsibility for any consequences arising from the use of this book, nor for
any material on third party websites, and cannot guarantee that any website address in this
book will be a suitable source of travel information. We value the views and suggestions of
our readers very highly. Please write to: Publisher, DK Eyewitness Travel Guides,
Dorling Kindersley, 80 Strand, London, Great Britain WC2R 0RL.

Left **Portoferraio, Elba** Centre **Tuscan shopkeeper** Right **Main piazza, Greve in Chianti**

Left **Michelangelo's** *David* Right **The hamlet of Montefioralle**

FLORENCE & TUSCANY'S TOP 10

FLORENCE & TUSCANY'S TOP 10

Florence & Tuscany's Highlights

Limiting the choice of prime sights to 10 is not an easy task in a land as rich and varied as Tuscany. Its storybook landscape is home to medieval hill towns, fabled wines and an unrivalled collection of Renaissance artistic masterpieces. Here are the best of the best.

1 The Uffizi, Florence
A veritable who's who of the greatest Renaissance masters installed in the former offices *(uffizi)* of the ruling Medici family *(see pp8–11)*.

2 The Duomo Group, Florence
Brunelleschi's noble dome, Giotto's slender belltower, Ghiberti's robust gates, Michelangelo's tortured *Pietà* and two panoramic terraces, all wrapped in red, white and green marble *(see pp12–13)*.

20 ⌐———— miles ⌐ 0 ⌐ km ————⌐ 20

3 Pitti Palace, Florence
Massive Medici palace with a painting collection to rival the Uffizi, museums of porcelain, carriages, and modern art, and formal gardens *(see pp14–17)*.

4 San Gimignano
A medieval fairy-tale town with stone towers and churches swathed in frescoes, surrounded by patch-work fields and terraced vineyards *(see pp18–21)*.

5 Campo dei Miracoli, Pisa

A grassy "Field of Miracles". The Campo is studded with masterpieces of Romanesque architecture: a Baptistry and Cathedral containing Gothic pulpits by Pisano and, of course, that ridiculously leaning, famous belltower *(see pp22–5)*.

6 Siena's Duomo

A striped giant of a cathedral stuffed with carvings, frescoes, Michelangelo's sculptures and Bernini's chapel *(see pp26–9)*.

Pistoia
Prato
Mugello
Casentino
Fiesole
1 2 3
Florence
Poppi
Pratomagno
Monte dei Chianti
San Gimignano 4
Chianti 8
Arezzo
Alpe della Luna
Volterra
Siena 6 7
Cortona 9
Callifere
San Galgano
Buonconvento
Ombrone
Massa Marittima
Chiusi
Grosseto
Saturnia
Pitigliano
Porto Santo Stefano
Isola del Giglio
Monte Argentario

7 Siena's Campo & Palazzo Pubblico

This sloping brick scallop shell is Siena's living room, its public palace a museum celebrating maestros of Gothic art *(see pp30–33)*.

8 Chianti

The ultimate Tuscan idyll, a landscape of hills clad in grape vines, topped by castles, and dotted with countryside *trattorie* serving Italy's most famous wine *(see pp34–7)*.

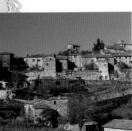

9 Cortona

Tuscany in miniature: medieval atmosphere, first-class art, sweeping views, handcrafted ceramics and fine wines *(see pp38–41)*.

10 Lucca

An elegant city of opera and arcaded Romanesque façades. The medieval towers and 16th-century ramparts are now domesticated as small parks *(see pp42–3)*.

🔟 The Uffizi, Florence

This museum is the ultimate primer on the Renaissance, starting with Giotto and running through Botticelli, Leonardo da Vinci, Michelangelo, Raphael, Titian, Caravaggio and beyond. This historic progression is only fitting, as the building, originally the uffizi ("offices") of the ruling Medici family, was designed by Giorgio Vasari, who wrote the world's first art history text. Some 1,700 works are on display, with another 1,400 in storage. Though small, these galleries shelter an embarrassing number of masterpieces that demand at least three or four hours.

Entrance

Café

Toilets

Arno façade of the Uffizi

🍽 The outdoor café is at the end of the west wing galleries, above the Loggia de Lanzi.

⏱ The queue to enter can last hours. Booking ahead is worth the small fee.

The Uffizi is undergoing major expansion involving layout changes until 2010. Pick up a gallery guide for the latest information.

• Piazzale degli Uffizi 6 (off Piazza della Signoria) • Map M–N4 • Ticket reservation 055 294 883 • www.uffizi.firenze.it
• 8:15am–6:50pm Tue–Sun (last entry 45 min before closing) Closed 1 Jan, 1 May, 25 Dec
• Admission charge

Top 10 Paintings

1. Birth of Venus (Botticelli)
2. The Annunciation (Leonardo da Vinci)
3. Holy Family (Michelangelo)
4. Maestà (Giotto)
5. Bacchus (Caravaggio)
6. Primavera (Botticelli)
7. Frederico di Montefeltro and Battista Sforza (Piero della Francesca)
8. Venus of Urbino (Titian)
9. Madonna of the Long Neck (Parmigianino)
10. Battle of San Romano (Uccelo)

Birth of Venus
Botticelli's Venus on a half shell, painted in 1486, is the ultimate Renaissance beauty. The pose is a classical Venus, while the face is said to be modelled on Simonetta Vespucci, the girlfriend of Piero de' Medici, and cousin to explorer Amerigo Vespucci.

The Annunciation
One of the earliest works (1475) of that versatile master Leonardo da Vinci. We can already see his attention to detail in the drapery and flower-bedecked lawn. Leonardo's patented *sfumato* landscape creates the illusion of great distance by introducing a hazy atmosphere.

Holy Family
A rare panel painting (1504) by Michelangelo, the *Holy Family* owes much to Signorelli, but its twisting figures, exotic saturated colours and lounging nudes predict Mannerism.

 For more museums in Tuscany See pp48–9

Maestà
Giotto's *Maestà* of 1310 is revolutionary compared with nearby similar scenes by his older contemporaries Duccio and Cimabue. Here the Madonna has bulk beneath her clothing, and depth is created through the placing of the surrounding figures on solid ground.

Primavera
Botticelli's companion to his *Birth of Venus*, the *Primavera* (1478; *above*) is populated by goddesses and over 500 species of plant. The painting's exact meaning is not known but it may be a Neoplatonic allegory of spring based around a poem by Poliziano.

Frederico di Montefeltro and Battista Sforza
Piero della Francesca's intense, psychological style of portraiture unflinchingly depicts his hook-nosed patron duke, literally warts and all.

Madonna of the Long Neck
Parmigianino's *Madonna* of 1534 shows off Mannerism at its twisted, exaggerated, elegant best, with an impossibly sinuous Madonna and a weirdly oversized infant Jesus. Though left unfinished, it would become a touchstone of the Mannerist movement and Parmigianino's masterpiece.

Battle of San Romano
A master of perspective, Uccello experimented with it to the detriment of his scenes. The broken lances in this third of his masterpiece (1456; other thirds are in Paris and London) over-define a perspective plane. Also, the background tilts at a radically different angle to the foreground.

Bacchus
One of Caravaggio's earliest works (1594) shows he is already marrying an intense attention to detail (evident in the Flemish-style still life of fruit), with earthy naturalism in the boy-like god. Also obvious is his early fascination with playing harsh light off deep shadows.

Venus of Urbino
A great influence on the depiction of the nude all the way through to Manet, Titian's *Venus of Urbino* (1538, *above*) was widely copied in the 18th and 19th centuries. The Venetian master also played with light and shadow, setting a luminous Venus against a dark background.

Museum Guide
Enter on the left (west) side of the U-shaped loggia opening off Piazza della Signoria; one entrance is for reserved tickets, the other for walk-ins. The galleries line the third floor's long corridor, rooms 2–24 in the east wing, 25–45 in the west. The room numbering isn't perfect (the walls between rooms 10–14 were removed long ago), and rooms 36–40 bore the brunt of the 1993 bombing and are closed.

For more on the Uffizi collections **See pp10–11**

Left *The Annunciation* detail Centre **Uffizi façade** Right *Madonna of the Goldfinch*, Raphael

10 The Uffizi: Collections

1 Botticelli (Rooms 10–14)
Tear your eyes away from the famed *Birth of Venus* and *Primavera (see pp8–9)* to peruse other Botticelli masterpieces such as *Pallas and the Centaur* and an *Adoration of the Magi* featuring a self-portrait (in yellow robes on the right). Compare that *Adoration* with those by Botticelli's student, Filippino Lippi, and by Botticelli's contemporary (and Michelangelo's teacher), Ghirlandaio.

2 Early Renaissance (Rooms 7–9)
The earthiness of Masaccio and the delicacy of Fra Angelico join the likes of Piero della Francesca and Paolo Uccello in Room 7. Renaissance ideals develop further with anatomically exacting works by the Pollaiuolo

brothers and the flowing lines of Masaccio's more elegant student Filippo Lippi (whose *Madonna and Child with Angels* is *below*). These lead up to the languid grace of Lippi's protégé, Botticelli.

3 Pre-Renaissance (Rooms 2–6)
The first Uffizi room bridges the medieval and proto-Renaissance with a trio of *Maestàs*, from Cimabue's Byzantine take, through Duccio's Sienese Gothic style, to Giotto's version *(see p9)*. Simone Martini's *Annunciation* represents the graceful 14th-century Sienese school. Gentile da Fabriano and Lorenzo Monaco give one final, colourful shout of the medieval in the International Gothic style of the early 1400s.

4 Leonardo da Vinci (Room 15)
Room 15 celebrates Verrocchio's star pupils, including Lorenzo di Credi, Botticini, Umbrian master Perugino (Raphael's teacher), and Leonardo da Vinci himself. As an apprentice, Leonardo painted the angel on the left of Verrocchio's *Baptism of Christ*. Leonardo da Vinci's *Annunciation (see p8)*, his unfinished, chaotic *Adoration of the Magi,* and Signorelli's *Crucifixion* round out the room.

5 High Renaissance and Mannerism
(Rooms 19, 25–32)
After some Peruginos, Signorellis and a Northern interlude, Room 25

For more about artists in Tuscany See pp50–51

Adoration of the Magi, Botticelli Collection

Floorplan: Collections

brings out the Renaissance big guns: Michelangelo and Raphael. Andrea del Sarto and his students developed Michelangelo's colours and asymmetrical positioning into Mannerism. Meanwhile, the High Renaissance Venetians Titian, Veronese and Tintoretto explored new realms of colour, light and composition.

Northern Italian and European Masters

(Rooms 20–23)
The works are fine but not outstanding. Northern Italian masters Bellini, Giorgione, Mantegna and Correggio are interspersed with their German and Flemish contemporaries Cranach, Holbein and Dürer. *Portrait of the Artist's Father* is Dürer's first work, painted at the age of 19. These rooms mostly provide a needed mental break before the High Renaissance collections.

Baroque (Rooms 33–44)

The Uffizi's post-Renaissance collections are not outstanding, save for a few by Caravaggio – *Bacchus (see p9)*, a *Sacrifice of Isaac* and *Medusa* – self-portraits by Rembrandt and Rubens, and Artemisia Gentileschi's gory *Judith and Holofernes.*

The Tribune (Room 18)

The Uffizi's original display space is a chamber with mother-of-pearl tiled-dome and inlaid *pietre dure* (stone) floor and table. It was built by Francesco I to show off the *Medici Venus* and other Classical statues. Portraits by Bronzino and Pontormo, Rosso Fiorentino's lute-plucking *Musician Angel,* and Raphael's *St John in the Desert* cover the walls.

Works in the U-shaped Corridor

The main corridor linking the galleries is lined with Classical statues – mostly Roman copies of Greek originals *(left).* Its ceiling vaults are frescoed (1581) with intricate grotesques celebrating Florence's history, thinkers, leaders and artists. Views from the short south corridor are justly celebrated.

Works in the Vasari Corridor

The kilometre- (half-mile-) long corridor between the Pitti Palace and Uffizi was damaged during a 1993 terrorist bombing. It is lined with works from the 17th to 20th centuries, including self-portraits, and open for booked guided tours for a limited period of the year.

For more Tuscan masterpieces **See pp52–3**

🔟 The Duomo Group, Florence

Florence's gorgeous cathedral offers two panoramic perches, one atop Giotto's lithe and lovely belltower, the other at the summit of Brunelleschi's robust and noble dome. The interior of the cathedral contains some Uccello frescoes but otherwise is oddly barren and less interesting than clambering up between the layers of the dome. The nearby Baptistry is also more rewarding with its glittering Byzantine mosaics and Gates of Paradise, while inside the Museo are statues by Michelangelo, Donatello, Ghirlandaio and Andrea Pisano.

Dome on Florence's Duomo

🍴 I Fratellini, four blocks down Via dei Calzaiuoli at Via dei Cimatori 38r, is a hole in the wall serving sandwiches and glasses of wine to patrons who eat standing on the cobblestone street.

🕐 The Baptistry opens at noon, so save the whole Duomo group for the afternoon.

The last ascent of the dome is 40 minutes before closing; queue early in summertime.

• Piazza del Duomo • Map M–N3 • Duomo open 10am–5pm Mon–Fri (to 3:30pm Thu), 10am–4:45pm Sat & Sun (from 1:30–4:45pm Sun) • Baptistry noon–7pm Mon–Sat, 8:30am–2pm Sun; admission charge €3 • Museo 9am–6:50pm daily (to 1pm Sun); €6 • Dome 8:30am–7pm Mon–Sat (to 5:40pm Sat); €6 • Campanile 8:30am–7:30pm daily; €6 • No cumulative ticket

Top 10 Features

1. Duomo: Dome
2. Baptistry: Gates of Paradise
3. Baptistry: Mosaics
4. Museo dell'Opera del Duomo Michelangelo's Pietà
5. Duomo: Campanile
6. Duomo: Fresco of Giovanni Acuto
7. Museo dell'Opera del Duomo: Habakkuk
8. Duomo: New Sacristy
9. Museo dell'Opera del Duomo: Altar Front
10. Baptistry: North Doors

Duomo: Dome

The Duomo's crossing was thought unspannable until Brunelleschi came up with this ingenious double shell construction in 1420. Forget the mediocre frescoes inside; the thrill is to climb up between the layers to the marble lantern at its peak.

Baptistry: Gates of Paradise

Lorenzo Ghiberti's gilded bronze panels (1425–53) showcase his mastery at depicting great depth in shallow relief *(right)*. Michelangelo was reportedly so moved he proclaimed they would "grace the very gates of Paradise", and the name stuck; the originals are housed in the Museo.

Baptistry: Mosaics

The swathe of 13th-century mosaic panels tells stories from Genesis and the lives of Jesus, Joseph and St John the Baptist.

For other churches in Florence See pp44–5

5 Duomo: Campanile

Giotto designed only the lowest level of the "Lily of Florence", which was continued by Andrea Pisano (who added statue niches) and finished by Francesco Talenti. It is 85 m (276 ft), or 414 steps, to the top.

6 Duomo: Fresco of Giovanni Acuto

Master of perspective Paolo Uccello painted this trompe-l'oeil fresco (1436) of an equestrian statue as a memorial for John Hawkwood, an English *condottiere* (mercenary commander) long in Florence's employ.

7 Museo dell'Opera del Duomo: Habakkuk

One of several prophets that Donatello carved for the campanile.

Lorenzo Ghiberti

Florentines nicknamed this one Lo Zuccone – "Pumpkinhead".

8 Duomo: New Sacristy

The bronze doors and glazed terracotta lunette are 15th-century works by Luca della Robbia. The interior, sheathed in wood inlay, was where Lorenzo de' Medici took refuge after an assassination attempt in 1478.

Museo dell'Opera: Michelangelo's Pietà 4

Michelangelo created three *Pietàs*, this middle one in 1548–55 before angrily attacking it with a hammer.

Duomo Plan

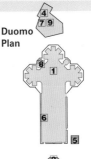

9 Museo dell'Opera del Duomo: Altar Front

This pile of silver and gilt statuary for the Baptistry took over 100 years to craft (1366–1480), by Verrocchio, Antonio Pollaiuolo, Michelozzo and other sculptors.

10 Baptistry: North Doors

Lorenzo Ghiberti won the 1401 competition to cast these 28 bronze panels, and spent 21 years creating what art historians consider the first proper Renaissance work.

Duomo History

The Baptistry was founded in the 6th century, but its structure is mostly 11th–14th-century. The massive cathedral itself wasn't started until 1294, when Arnolfo di Cambio began building around the diminutive old Santa Reparata. The Duomo was largely finished by 1417; in 1420–36 Brunelleschi's innovative engineering added the dome, topped by Verrocchio's bronze ball in the 1460s. The overwrought façade is 19th-century Neo-Gothic.

For churches outside Florence **See pp46–7**

Pitti Palace, Florence

This one-time residence of the Medici family is a treasure trove: there are royal apartments, galleries of modern art, costume, silverware and porcelain. But above all there is the Galleria Palatina, frescoed by Pietro da Cortona, and second only to the Uffizi. It contains one of the world's best collections of Raphaels and Titians. The paintings are still hung 19th-century style, when "Does that Tintoretto match the room's decor?" or "Let's put all the round ones together" mattered more than any didactic arrangement.

Façade of the Pitti Palace

○ Wine bar Pitti Gola e Cantina, at Piazza Pitti 16, also offers light meals.

○ Picnics are not officially allowed in the Boboli Gardens.

If you liked the Pitti's *pietre dure* table *(see p17)*, buy a modern version at a shop on the Piazza Pitti called Pitti Mosaici.

• Piazza dei Pitti
• Map L5 • Galleria Palatina and Appartamenti Reali: 055 294 883, open 8:15am–6:50pm Tue–Sun
• Galleria del Costume, open 8:15am–6:50pm, closed 2nd and 4th Sun and 1st, 3rd and 5th Mon of each month • Museo della Porcellana, Museo degli Argenti & Boboli Gardens: open Nov–Feb: 8:15am–4:30pm; Mar: 8:15am–5:30pm; Apr–May, Sep–Oct: 8:15am–6:30pm; Jun–Aug: 8:15am–7:30pm daily. Closed 1st and last Mon of month
• Admission charge; some cumulative tickets available

Top 10 Pitti Sights

1. La Velata (Raphael)
2. Consequences of War (Rubens)
3. Mary Magdalene (Titian)
4. Boboli Gardens
5. Madonna and Child (Lippi)
6. Three Ages of Man (Giorgione)
7. Green Room of the Royal Apartments
8. Ammanati's Courtyard
9. Tuscan Maremma (Fattori)
10. Grotta Grande

La Velata

Raphael did many portraits, usually of Madonnas, and several of his best are in these collections. *La Velata* (1516) is his masterpiece of the form, demonstrating his mastery of colour, light and form. The sitter is most likely La Fornarina, Raphael's Roman girlfriend.

Consequences of War

Venus tries to stop Mars going to war, while a Fate pulls him towards it (1638; *right*). This was an ageing Rubens's plea against his homeland becoming embroiled in the Thirty Years' War (1618–48).

Mary Magdalene

The first (1535) of many Mary Magdalenes painted by the Venetian master Titian.

Boboli Gardens

The Renaissance garden with Baroque and Rococo touches has cypress avenues, hidden statues and burbling fountains.

For more on the Galleria Palatina **See pp16–17**

5 Madonna and Child

Filippo Lippi has masterfully placed the Madonna's chin in this 1450 painting's geometric centre, helping to unite a complex composition involving both the main scene and background images from the life of the Virgin.

Key to Plan

- Galleria Palatina
- Palace
- Gardens

6 Three Ages of Man

The attribution of this allegorical work of 1500 to Giorgione is not certain, but it is a beautiful piece nonetheless, with a strong sense of colour and composition. Compare it with the Baroque *Four Ages of Man* (1637), which was frescoed by Pietro da Cortona on the ceiling of the Sala della Stufa.

7 Green Room, the Royal Apartments

The best-preserved room in the royal apartments (Appartamenti Reali) contains such lavish furnishings as an ebony cabinet inlaid with semi-precious stones and bronze. The ceiling of the Green Room is set with trompe l'oeil stuccoes and a canvas by Luca Giordano.

8 Ammannati's Courtyard

Mannerist architecture was a robust, oversized retake on the Renaissance. Bartolomeo Ammannati expounded this in dramatic, heavily rusticated Classical orders (1560–70).

9 The Tuscan Maremma

On the second floor, the modern art museum's masterpiece is a work (1850) by Giovanni Fattori. He was the greatest of the Macchaioli, a 19th-century Tuscan school with parallels to Impressionism.

10 Grotta Grande

Mannerist cavern dripping with stylized stalactites, Giambologna statues and plaster casts of Michelangelo's *Slaves*.

Museum Guide

You enter through Ammannati's Courtyard (the ticket office is to the right of Pitti Palace). Galleria Palatina and Appartamenti Reali are on the first floor, but see the Palatina first. The entrance to the Boboli is in the back right-hand corner. The other collections, in order of interest, are: Modern Art Gallery (second floor), Costume Gallery (in the Meridiana Summer Palace, also entered via the Boboli), Silver Collection (ground floor), Carriage Museum (in the left wing – but closed until further notice), and the Porcelain Museum (at the top of the Boboli).

For more on the Medici family See pp54–5

Left **Galleria Palatina** Centre **Ammannati's Courtyard** Right **Pitti Palace façade**

Pitti Palace: Galleria Palatina

Sala di Giove

This room holds two Pitti Top 10s: Raphael's *La Velata* and Giorgione's *Three Ages of Man*. Early Renaissance masterpieces include Perugino's *Madonna del Sacco*, a subtle study of spatial relationships, and a small, wrinkly *St Jerome* either by Verrocchio or Piero di Pollaiuolo. Andrea del Sarto painted *St John the Baptist* (1523) in a Classical style, but his *Annunciation* (1512) is proto-Mannerist. Fra' Bartolomeo's *Lamentation of the Dead Christ* (1512) and Bronzino's *Guidobaldo Della Rovere* (1532) are High Renaissance works that anticipate the Baroque.

Sala di Saturno

Raphael's entire career is covered here, from the Leonardesque *Madonna del Granduca* (1506) to his late *Vision of Ezekiel* (1518). Among his other Madonnas and portraits, seek out the Mona Lisa-inspired *Maddalena Doni* (1506), which heavily influenced Renaissance portraiture. Raphael's Umbrian teacher Perugino painted a strikingly composed *Lamentation of the Dead Christ* (1495). Fra' Bartolomeo's *Stupor Mundi* (1516) and del Sarto's fresh *Annunciation and Dispute of the Trinity* (1517) then round out the room.

Sala di Apollo

Titian finds a home here: his *Mary Magdalene (below)* hangs near his *Portrait of an Englishman* (1540). Influential works abound: Andrea del Sarto's *Pietà* (1522) and *Holy Family* (1523) helped found the Mannerist style. The tight, focused power of the *Sacred Conversation* (1522), by del Sarto's student Rosso Fiorentino, was affected when the painting was later artificially extended to fit a large Baroque frame. The Classical style of Bolognese artists Guido Reni (a late *Cleopatra*) and Guercino (an early *Resurrection of Tabitha*) helped inform the burgeoning Baroque.

Sala di Venere

The centrepiece of the room is a *Venus* carved by Canova to replace the ancient original Napoleon had shipped to Paris (now in the Uffizi). Titian steals the

For more great museums See pp48–9

show with *The Concert* (1510; his elder, Giorgione, may have contributed), a *Portrait of Julius II* (1545) copied from Raphael, and the celebrated *Portrait of Pietro Aretino* (1545). Rubens's bucolic *Return from the Hayfields* is often overlooked.

Sala di Marte
Rubens dominates with *The Consequences of War* (1638) and *Four Philosophers* (1612), which includes portraits of himself (far left) and his brother. The fine portrait collection includes the penetrating *Portrait of a Man* (1550), which is attributed to Veronese, *Luigi Conaro* (1560), which is now attributed to Tintoretto, *Ippolito de' Medici* (1532) by Titian and *Cardinal Bentivoglio* by Van Dyck.

Later Works
After Napoleon's Bathroom, the quality really peters out, though the names – Tintoretto, Rubens, Botticelli, Pontormo – remain major. The only masterworks are Raphael's *Madonna dell'Impannata* (1514) and a Filippo Lippi *Madonna and Child* (1450), the museum's oldest painting. Compare Signorelli's *Sacra Famiglia*, which influenced Michelangelo's in the Uffizi, with that of Beccafumi – a Mannerist take informed by Michelangelo's work.

Sala dell'Illiade
Raphael's unusual, almost Flemish-style portrait of a pregnant woman, *La Gravida* (1506), is the star of the room. Andrea del Sarto is represented by a pair of *Assumptions* (1523 and 1526). Artemisia Gentileschi is also represented: she was the

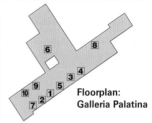

Floorplan: Galleria Palatina

Baroque's only noted female artist and often portrayed strong female biblical characters, including *Mary Magdalene* and *Judith*, in her works.

Galleria delle Statue
Paintings are on temporary display in this long entrance hall, but a few have been here for years, including Caravaggio's violent genre scene *The Toothpuller* (officially an Uffizi painting), and an early Rubens *Risen Christ*. Don't miss the gorgeous 19th-century table in *pietre dure* – the Florentine art of inlaid stone.

Sala dell'Educazione di Giove
Two works of particular note here: Caravaggio's *Sleeping Cupid* (1608) is a study in realism and chiaroscuro. Christofano Allori's *Judith Beheading Holofernes* has double meanings: every face is a portrait. Judith is the artist's girlfriend, the old woman looking on bears the face of her mother, and Holofernes' decapitated head is Allori's self-portrait.

Sala della Stufa and Napoleon's Bathroom
The Sala della Stufa preserves Pietro da Cortona frescoes and 1640 majolica flooring. Napoleon's Empire-style bathroom is one of the few Pitti remnants of the Frenchman's brief Italian reign.

Venus, Sala di Venere

For more sights in Florence **See pp76–83**

🔟 San Gimignano

Souvenir shops notwithstanding, this pedestrianized hilltop town is the most evocative of the Middle Ages of any in Tuscany. Its full name is San Gimignano delle Belle Torri, or San Gimignano of the Beautiful Towers. More than 70 of these towers once attested to this medieval Manhattan's wealth; 14 still spike its skyline today. The town boasts, for its size, an amazing wealth of 14th- and 15th-century art. Modern art, too, is tucked into unexpected corners, and there is an excellent local white wine.

Piazza della Cisterna

Ceiling of the Collegiata

🍦 Bar I Combattenti (Via San Giovanni 124) serves the best *gelato* in town.

🚌 The tour buses leave around 5pm: spend the night to enjoy the town like a local.

- Map D3 • Tourist office on Piazza del Duomo 1
- 0577 940 008 • www.sangimignano.com •
Collegiata open daily (closed 27 Jan–28 Feb); admission charge €3.50
- Museo Civico open daily; admission €5 •
Museo della Tortura open daily; admission €8
- Museo Archeologico open daily; admission €3.50 • Museo d'Arte Sacra open daily Mar–Dec; admission €3
- Cumulative tickets are available from the tourist office

Top 10 Sights

1. Collegiata
2. Torre Grossa
3. Museo Civico
4. Piazza della Cisterna
5. Sant'Agostino
6. Museo della Tortura
7. Museo Archeologico
8. Museo d'Arte Sacra
9. Rocca
10. Façade of San Francesco

❶ Collegiata

The plain exterior belies an interior swathed in frescoes. Lippo Memmi executed those on the right wall (1333–41), Bartolo di Fredi the left wall (1367), Taddeo di Bartolo the gory *Last Judgement* in the nave (1410), and Benozzo Gozzoli the entrance wall's *St Sebastian* (1464). The town's pride are the Domenico Ghirlandaio frescoes (1475) in the Chapel of Santa Fina.

❷ Torre Grossa

You can climb all 54 m (175 ft) of the tallest tower in town for one of Italy's most stupendous views, across the surrounding towers and terracotta roofs to the rolling hills all around.

❸ Museo Civico

San Gimignano's best museum is situated on the first floor of the Palazzo del Popolo, beneath the lofty Torre Grossa. The collection includes works by Pinturicchio (whose *Madonna with Saints Gregory and Benedict*, 1511, is pictured left), Filippino Lippi and Benozzo Gozzoli, and a *Maestà* by Lippo Memmi. The frescoes (by Memmo di Filuppucci) of a couple's marriage and wedding night are unusually erotic for the 14th century.

Piazza della Cisterna

This triangular piazza *(left)*, ringed with 13th- and 14th-century towers and centred on a 1237 stone well, will be familiar as a setting for such films as *Where Angels Fear to Tread* and *Tea with Mussolini*.

Museo Archeologico

The small collection of Etruscan artifacts housed here includes a curious funerary urn topped by a reclining effigy of the deceased, his cup holding a coin to pay for entry into the afterlife.

Rocca

The 14th-century fortress has long since crumbled to a romantic ruin, and is now planted with olives and figs. Scramble up its ramparts for a picture-perfect view of the town's towers.

Façade of San Francesco

The Romanesque façade of a long-vanished church remains wedged between later medieval buildings. Behind it is a local vineyard's *cantina*, offering wine tastings, and, beyond, a pretty, shaded terrace with fine country views.

Sant'Agostino

Most tourists miss this little church with its Piero di Pollaiuolo altarpiece (1483) and Benozzo Gozzoli's quirky, colourful apse frescoes on the life of St Augustine (1465). Benedetto da Maiano carved the tomb of San Bartolo (1488) against the west wall.

Museo della Tortura

A grisly array of torture instruments occupies the Torre della Diavola (She-devil's Tower). The explanatory placards make for grim reading, pointing out which of the devices are still used around the world today.

Museo d'Arte Sacra

This modest museum of liturgical art *(below)* stands on a pretty piazza off the Collegiata's left flank. Highlights of the collection are a *Madonna and Child* by Bartolo di Fredi and 14th-century illuminated choir books.

San Gimignano's History

The Etruscan and later Roman settlement blossomed as a stop-off on the medieval Francigena pilgrimage route. Competing families erected the towers – partly for show, partly for defence during their street battles. The devastating 1348 plague left the town under Florentine control, and the Francigena shifted east. San Gimignano became a backwater, its medieval character preserved to this day.

🔟 Campo dei Miracoli, Pisa

Pisa's "Field of Miracles" is one of the most gorgeous squares in Italy, its green carpet of grass the setting for the Pisan-Romanesque gemstones of the Duomo, Baptistry, Camposanto and Campanile – that Italian icon better known as the Leaning Tower. The east end of the square is anchored by the old bishop's palace, now home to the Duomo museum. Souvenir stalls cling like barnacles to the long south side of the square; a doorway between two of them opens into the Museo delle Sinopie, housing the giant preparatory sketches on plaster for the lost Camposanto frescoes.

The Tower and beyond

🥪 **Il Canguro, Via Santa Maria 151, is a great sandwich shop: take your drink and panino back to the lawns of Campo dei Miracoli to picnic.**

🕐 **The opening times of sites vary: check with the tourist office.**

The Duomo is closed on Sundays, but you can still see it if you attend mass.

• Map C3 • Tourist office: Via C. Cammeo 2
• 050 560 464 • Campo dei Miracoli: 050 387 2210; www.opapisa.it
• Duomo open Mon–Sat; admission charge €2 (free Nov–Feb)
• Baptistry open daily; €5 • Camposanto open daily; €5 • Museo del Duomo open daily; €5
• Museo delle Sinopie open daily; €5 • Tower €15, other sites: €5 for one, €6 for two, €10 for five; €2 city walls

Top 10 Sights

1. Leaning Tower
2. Baptistry
3. Baptistry Pulpit
4. Duomo Façade
5. Duomo's San Ranieri Doors
6. Duomo Pulpit
7. Camposanto
8. Camposanto Triumph of Death fresco
9. Museo dell'Opera del Duomo
10. Museo delle Sinopie

Leaning Tower
1 This belltower in the Pisan-Romanesque style was begun in 1173 and started leaning when builders were only on the third level: the weight was too much for the alluvial subsoil. By 1990, the tower was 4.5 m (15 ft) out of vertical, and it was closed until 2001 for engineers to reverse the tilt. Entrance is accompanied (30 people admitted every half hour).

Baptistry
2 Italy's largest Baptistry *(right)* started life as a Romanesque piece (1153) but has a Gothic dome. The acoustically perfect interior houses a great Gothic pulpit.

Baptistry Pulpit
3 Niccola Pisano's Gothic masterpiece (1255–60; *above*) depicts religious scenes based on pagan reliefs decorating Camposanto sarcophagi.

Duomo Façade
4 A Pisan-Romanesque triumph *(above)* of blind arcades, stacked open arcades and coloured marble decorations. Mannerist artist Giambologna cast the bronze doors to replace those destroyed by fire in 1595.

For other sights in Pisa See pp24–5

5 Duomo's San Ranieri Doors

The architect Buscheto sculpted the only remaining Romanesque bronze doors of Pisa's cathedral in 1180. He populated them with minimalist biblical scenes and swaying palm trees.

6 Duomo Pulpit

Niccola Pisano's son, Giovanni, carved this in 1302–11. The Gothic naturalism of its tumultuous New Testament scenes probably reflects the influence of Giotto, who was a contemporary of the artist in Padua.

Plan of the Campo dei Miracoli

7 Camposanto

This former cemetery, containing recycled ancient Roman sarcophagi, once boasted frescoes to rival those in the Sistine Chapel. They were largely destroyed in World War II, but a few sections are preserved in a back room.

9 Museo dell'Opera del Duomo

This rich collection includes an 11th-century Islamic bronze hippogriff (half horse, half griffin, *above*) – Crusade booty that once topped the cathedral dome. Good Leaning Tower views, too.

10 Museo delle Sinopie

In trying to salvage the Camposanto frescoes, restorers discovered earlier preparatory sketches. These offer a unique insight into the creative process of these medieval artists.

8 Camposanto Triumph of Death Fresco

This fresco *(left)* by Buffamalcco is the best of those that survived the bombs of World War II. Its scene of Death riding across an apocalyptic landscape inspired Liszt to compose his *Totentanz* concerto.

Orientation

The Campo is a bus ride (numbers 1, 3 or 11) from Pisa Centrale station or a short walk from San Rossore station. Admission to the sites comes in several configurations, currently: a ticket for the Duomo alone; any one, two or five sites, except the Duomo and Tower; any two sites; everything save the Duomo; everything except the Tower; and the Tower alone.

Left **S Caterina** Centre left **Piazza d' Cavalieri** Centre right **Vettovaglie Market** Right **Museo San Matteo**

Other Pisan Sights

Museo San Matteo

Often-overlooked collection of 13th-century Crucifixions and such notable works as Simone Martini's *Virgin and Child with Saints* (1321; *above*), Nino Pisano's *Madonna del Latte* and Donatello's bust of San Rossore. Masaccio, Fra Angelico, Gozzoli, Lorenzo di Credi and Ghirlandaio are also represented.

Santa Maria della Spina

A pinnacled jewel of Gothic architecture *(right)* built in 1230–1323 by Nino and Giovanni Pisano to house a thorn said to be from Christ's crown, brought back by a Pisan Crusader.

Piazza Vettovaglie Market

This attractive arcaded piazza stands at the centre of Pisa's colourful, lively outdoor food market.

Piazza dei Cavalieri

The probable site of the ancient forum is ringed by Giorgio Vasari's sgrafitto façade on the Palazzo dei Cavalieri (1562), the baroque Santo Stefano and the Palazzo dell'Orologio. It was in the latter's tower that Count Ugolino – immortalized by Dante and Shelley – was locked away to starve with his sons in 1288, accused of treason.

Le Navi Antiche di Pisa

Ten Roman ships, dating from 100 BC to AD 400 and probably sunk by flash floods or storms, were discovered in 1998 during work on San Rossore station (which was the harbour area before the Arno silted up). The ships' cargo and everyday accoutrements are displayed in the Medici Arsenale as they are excavated, and will eventually be joined by the ships themselves.

For shopping and eating in Pisa **See pp110–11**

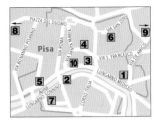

Santa Caterina

Behind the 1330 Gothic façade hides Nino Pisano's *Annunciation* and his tomb of Simone Saltarelli (1342), as well as Francesco Triani's *Apothesis of St Thomas Aquinas* (1350).

San Paolo a Ripa d'Arno

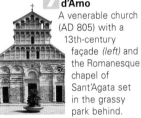

A venerable church (AD 805) with a 13th-century façade *(left)* and the Romanesque chapel of Sant'Agata set in the grassy park behind.

Tenuta di San Rossore

Coastal wildlife reserve, with boar, deer and waterfowl. The poet Shelley's body was washed ashore here in 1822 after his supposed murder by pirates.

Certosa di Calci

This Carthusian monastery of 1366, 12 km (8 miles) east of town, is stuffed with Baroque frescoed chapels and cloisters.

San Nicola

The 1,000-year-old church *(right)* has a belltower staircase that inspired Donato Bramante's Vatican steps.

The Leaning Tower

The belfry

Italy's most famous symbol, stamped on pizza boxes the world over, leans a staggering 15 feet (4.5 m) out of plumb. The problem: 55 m (180 ft) of marble stacked atop watery, alluvial sand. A worrisome list developed soon after building started in 1173. Work stopped until 1275, when it was decided to curve the tower back as it rose (catch it at a certain angle and it looks like a banana). By 1990, with over a million tourists annually tramping up the tower, collapse seemed imminent. The tower was closed, with restraining bands strapped around it, lead weights stacked on one side and the base excavated to try to reverse the lean. It eventually reopened, for accompanied visits only, at the end of 2001.

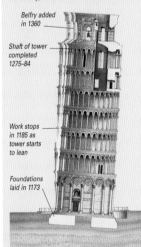

Belfry added in 1360

Shaft of tower completed 1275–84

Work stops in 1185 as tower starts to lean

Foundations laid in 1173

The Tower's Foundations

The tower rests on a stone platform. An attempt was made in 1836 to dig out the foundations, but the lean worsened. A new concrete sleeve and draining the water table have helped.

For more on Northwestern Tuscany **See pp106–11**

🔟 Siena's Duomo

Siena's hulking Gothic cathedral is a treasure house of late Gothic sculpture, early Renaissance painting and Baroque design. The early architects dressed the edifice in striking Romanesque stripes, but the form is firmly Gothic, one of the best examples of the style in Italy. Equally fascinating are the Duomo's outbuildings: the Baptistry, the Museo Metropolitana and the Santa Maria della Scala hospital across the square, where 1440s frescoes on the walls of the wards depict medieval hospital scenes.

Duomo façade

🟢 Bini, Via dei Fusari 9–13, is a traditional bakery that has been producing heavenly Sienese cookies and sweets since 1943.

✪ Though the Duomo's floor panels by Beccafumi are usually covered for protection, you can see his detailed preparatory drawings at the Pinacoteca *(see p87)*.

A cumulative ticket saves on admission to the Library, Museo Metropolitana and Baptistry.

• All sights open daily: Duomo & Library 10:30am–7:30pm Mon–Sat, 1:30–5:30pm Sun (to 8pm Jun–Aug); Museo 9:30am–7pm (to 8pm Jun–Aug). Baptistry 9:30am–7pm (to 8pm Jun–Aug). Santa Maria della Scala 10:30am–6:30pm
• Admission charge €3 for Library

Top 10 Features

1. Pisano Pulpit
2. Piccolomini Library
3. Floor Panels
4. Façade
5. Piccolomini Altar
6. Chigi Chapel
7. San Giovanni Chapel
8. Duccio's Stained Glass Window
9. Choir
10. Belltower

Pisano Pulpit

Niccola Pisano's son, Giovanni, and pupil Arnolfo di Cambio helped create this masterpiece of Gothic carving. Similar to Pisano pulpits in Pisa and Pistoia, this one depicts scenes from the Life of Christ.

Floor panel

Piccolomini Library

The library was built to house manuscripts belonging to the humanist Pope Pius II, born to Siena's Piccolomini family. His life is celebrated in masterly frescoes (1507; left) by Pinturicchio.

For more on Siena **See pp86–91**

Floor Panels

All 59 panels are on show in early autumn (usually September), but some are visible all year. From 1372 to 1547 Siena's top artists created these scenes, including Pinturicchio and Matteo di Giovanni, whose *Massacre of the Innocents (below)* is masterful.

Piccolomini Altar

Andrea Bregno's 1480 marble altar incorporates a *Madonna and Child (1397–1400)* by Jacopo della Quercia and four small statues of saints (1501–4) by the young Michelangelo.

Chigi Chapel

Baroque master Gian Lorenzo Bernini designed this chapel in 1659. The 13th-century *Madonna del Volto* altarpiece is Siena's guardian: officials have placed the city keys before her in times of crisis, including during Nazi occupation, and Siena has always been delivered from harm.

San Giovanni Chapel

Giovanni di Stefano's Renaissance baptismal chapel (1492) is decorated with Pinturicchio frescoes and a bronze *St John the Baptist* (1457) by an ageing Donatello.

Duccio's Stained Glass Window

Italy's earliest stained glass (1288) decorates the apse's round window. Designed by Siena's great early Gothic master Duccio di Buoninsegna, it underwent a thorough cleaning in the 1990s and the original has now been placed in the Museo Metropolitana.

Façade

Giovanni Pisano designed the façade *(right)* in 1285. His original time-worn statues, replaced with copies, are in the Museo Metropolitana. The glittering mosaics decorating the top half are by 19th-century Venetian craftsmen.

Duomo Floor Plan

Choir

The intarsia wood choir stalls are by various master craftsmen (1362–1570), the marble altar by Baldassare Peruzzi (1532) and the candelabras by Beccafumi, who also painted the apse fresco of the *Ascension* (1548–51).

Belltower

The campanile was added only in 1313, but the design is pure Romanesque dramatic black-and-white stripes.

History of the Duomo

The Duomo was largely built between 1215 and 1263 by, among others, Nicola Pisano. His son Giovanni designed the façade. In 1339 work began on a massive new nave, the intention being to turn the Duomo we see today into merely the transept of the largest cathedral in Christendom. The 1348 Black Death thwarted the plan, however, and the unfinished nave wall now houses the Museo Metropolitana. The would-be façade is now a panoramic terrace.

For more Tuscan churches See pp44–7

Left **Pinturicchio fresco, Duomo** Centre **Duomo statue overlooking the Piazza** Right **Duomo façade**

Sights on the Piazza del Duomo

1 Museo Metropolitana: Duccio's Maestà
The heavyweight masterpiece of Sienese Gothic painting. When Duccio finished it in 1311, Siena's citizens paraded it through the streets to the Duomo's altar.

2 Baptistry Font (1417–30)
The brilliant bronze *Life of the Baptist* panels were cast a generation before painters discovered perspective.

3 Museo Metropolitana: Panorama from "Façade"
The Museo inhabits what would have been the nave wall of the Duomo's aborted 14th-century expansion *(see p27)*. Climb tight spiral stairs to the top of that never-realized church's unfinished "façade" for great views of the city.

4 Museo Metropolitana: Madonna and Child
This is Donatello's masterpiece of his *schiacciato* technique,

Santa Maria della Scala

Plan of the Piazza del Duomo

combining an etched perspective background with severely distorted (when seen close-to) high relief, to create the illusion of great depth in a nearly flat surface.

5 Santa Maria della Scala: Sala del Pellegrino
The former hospital ward features 1440s scenes by Domenico di Bartolo, including monks tending the sick. The symbolic orphans climbing a ladder *(scala)* to heaven are by Vecchietta.

6 Museo Metropolitana: Birth of the Virgin
This richly coloured, highly detailed Gothic work by Pietro Lorenzetti uses real arches to introduce trompe l'oeil painted ceiling vaults, creating a sense of deep space.

7 Baptistry: Ceiling Frescoes
Gaze heavenwards in the Baptistry and marvel at the

For more on Tuscan art and artists **See pp50–51**

dense frescoes by Vecchietta (1440s); note the inclusion of such delightful details as a monstrous crocodile.

Museo Archeologico
A small but worthwhile collection, including Greek vases from Southern Italy, Etruscan bronzes and alabaster urns, and Roman coins.

Santa Maria della Scala: Meeting at Porta Andrea
This work of 1512 by the Mannerist painter Beccafumi is full of his trademark odd colours and weird lighting.

Sun symbol, Piazza del Duomo

Santa Maria della Scala: Oratorio di Santa Caterina della Notte
Small basement oratory featuring a sumptuous Gothic altarpiece (1400) by Taddeo di Bartolo.

Top 10 Relics in Tuscany
1. Virgin's Girdle (Prato, Duomo, *see p47*)
2. Volto Santo (Lucca, Duomo)
3. Thorn from Christ's Crown (Pisa, Santa Maria della Spina)
4. Madonna del Voto (Siena, Duomo)
5. Head of St Cecilia (Siena, San Domenico)
6. Crucifix (Florence, Santa Trinità)
7. Piece of the True Cross (Impruneta, Collegiata)
8. Sword in the Stone (San Galgano, *see p114*)
9. Rib of a Dragon (Tirli)
10. Galileo's Finger (Florence, Science Museum)

The Virgin's Girdle
The country that gave the world Roman Catholicism is rich in artefacts imbued with miraculous qualities. Here, a girdle said to have been worn by the Virgin is brought to Italy by boat in 1141.

Miracles and Relics

The nave of Santa Trinità

Miracles have punctuated history in this fervently Christian land of saints and holy relics. When the crucifix in Florence's Santa Trinità nodded its head to nobleman Giovanni Gualberto in 1028, he founded the Vallombrosan monastic order. The miraculous powers of the Madonna frescoes in a Florence granary and a Prato prison assured the buildings' transformations into the churches of Orsanmichele and Santa Maria delle Carceri. When the Crusader who brought the Virgin's girdle back to Prato selfishly hid it under his mattress, angels levitated his bed, retrieved the relic and flew it to the bishop. San Galgano even has a bona fide sword in the stone, plunged there by a soldier after St Michael appeared to him, ordering him to renounce his warrior ways and become a holy hermit.

Siena's Campo & Palazzo Pubblico

The Piazza del Campo is often referred to affectionately as Il Campo. It is one of Europe's loveliest squares, where crowds turn out to stroll, gossip or picnic. It has been the centre of Sienese public life since it was laid out atop the city's Roman Forum in 1100. The governmental Palazzo Pubblico, with its graceful tower, was added in 1297, and the curve of brick buildings opposite built to match. The Palazzo houses the Museo Civico (see pp32–3). Twice a year the Campo is packed with crowds for the bareback Palio horse race (see pp66–7).

The Campo from the air

Several pricey cafés and restaurants ring the Campo (sometimes worth it for the pleasure of sipping a cappuccino at an outdoor table). Siena's top café, Nannini, is just north of the Campo at Via Banchi di Sopra 22–4.

There's a tiny, basic grocery store a few doors down Via di Salicotto on the left, where you can get picnic supplies and then stake out a prime Campo spot.

• Tourist Office: Piazza del Campo 56; 0577 280 551; www.comune. siena.it • Palazzo Pubblico (home of the Museo Civico) open summer: 10am–7pm daily (winter: until 5:30pm); admission charge €7 • Torre del Mangia open 10am–4pm daily (to 7pm mid-Mar–Oct) admission charge €7 • Palazzo Piccolomini open 9am–1pm Mon–Sat

Top 10 Sights

1. Palazzo Pubblico: Fresco Cycle
2. Palazzo Pubblico: Guidoriccio da Foligno (Simone Martini)
3. Piazza il Campo
4. Torre del Mangia
5. Cappella della Piazza
6. Fonte Gaia
7. Palazzo Pubblico
8. Loggia della Mercanzia
9. Palazzo Piccolomini
10. Palazzo Sansedoni

Palazzo Pubblico: Fresco Cycle
Ambrogio Lorenzetti's *Allegory of Good and Bad Government* (1338), the greatest secular medieval fresco cycle in Europe, decorates the old city council chamber.

Palazzo Pubblico: Guidoriccio da Foligno
This work of 1330 *(below)* is Simone Martini's greatest – though some challenge its authorship. The austere Maremma landscape, where Guidoriccio has just quashed a rebellion, is charming.

Piazza il Campo
The square's nine sections honour the medieval ruling Council of Nine. Its fountain and slope are more than decorative: they're integral to the city's water system.

Torre del Mangia
One of the tallest medieval towers in Italy, at 102 m (336 ft). There are 503 steps to the top – worth the effort for the stunning view.

5 Cappella della Piazza

When the Black Death of 1348 finally abated, the third of Sienese citizens who survived built this marble loggia to give thanks for their deliverance – and to pray against a repeat of the plague. A detail of its pretty stone carving is illustrated here.

Campo & Palazzo Plan

9 Palazzo Piccolomini

Housed in Siena's only Florentine Renaissance palazzo are the Tavolette di Biccherna – municipal ledgers from the 13th century, with covers by Sano di Pietro, Ambrogio Lorenzetti, Domenico Beccafumi and others.

10 Palazzo Sansedoni

The oldest building on the Campo; its curving 13th-century façade set the style for the rest of the square.

6 Fonte Gaia

The felicitous "Fountain of Joy" is pretty enough, but it is merely a mediocre 19th-century reproduction of the original, whose weathered carvings by Jacopo della Quercia are preserved in the Museo Civico *(see p32)*.

7 Palazzo Pubblico

The city's civic palace (1297–1310; *right*), with its graceful brickwork, Gothic three-light windows and thoroughly medieval crenellations, set the standard for Sienese architecture. Its sumptuously decorated rooms are now part of the civic museum.

8 Loggia della Mercanzia

A commercial tribunal once held court under this 1417 loggia *(above)* decorated with statues by Vecchietta and Federighi. The judges were so famously impartial that governments from across Europe brought their financial disputes to be heard here.

Siena's Contrade

The Campo is common ground for Siena's 17 traditional *contrade*, or wards. The Sienese are citizens of their *contrada* first, Siena second and Italy third. They are baptized in the *contrada* church, and should marry within their *contrada*; the *contrada* helps them in business, acts as their social club and mourns their passing like family. The *contrade* do not tolerate crime, giving Siena one of Europe's lowest crime rates. Inter-*contrade* rivalries are played out on the Campo in the annual Palio horse race.

For more architectural masterpieces **See p53**

Detail of frescoes, Sala del Mappamondo

Siena's Museo Civico

Sala della Pace
Contains medieval Europe's greatest secular fresco, full of everyday life details *(see p30)*.

Sala del Mappamondo
Across from Simone Martini's *Guidoriccio da Foligno* *(see also p30)* is his impressive *Maestà* (1315). Among the frescoes is a monochrome 15th-century battle scene.

Anticappella and Cappella
Taddeo di Bartolo frescoed both rooms. The chapel, beyond an ornate screen, contains a fine altarpiece by Sodoma.

Sala di Balia
Spinello Aretino and his son teamed up (1407–08) to illustrate the life of Pope Alexander III, featuring a fantastic naval battle.

Floor Plan

Sala del Risorgimento
The room boasts 19th-century sculptures and murals on the life of King Vittorio Emanuele II, who unified Italy.

Loggia
The weathered remnants of Jacopo della Quercia's Fonte Gaia sculptures (1409–19) rest under the timbers of this open loggia.

Sala del Concistoro
Bored delegates at government meetings can gaze at ceiling frescoes by Beccafumi.

Anticamera del Concistoro
An Ambrogio Lorenzetti fresco is among the treasures here.

Vestibule
It is only a passageway, but it houses a 1429 gilded bronze she-wolf honouring Siena's Roman origins, and a fresco by Ambrogio Lorenzetti.

16th- to 18th-Century Paintings
These are the first rooms you come to, but are probably the least interesting of them all!

Palazzo Pubblico, home of the Museo Civico

Top 10 Sienese Artists

1. Simone Martini (1284–1344)
2. Duccio di Buoninsegna (1260–1319)
3. Ambrogio Lorenzetti (active 1319–48)
4. Pietro Lorenzetti (active 1306–48)
5. Domenico Beccafumi (1484–1551)
6. Sodoma (Giovanni Antonio Bazzi; 1477–1549)
7. Jacopo della Quercia (1371–1438)
8. Sassetta (1390–1450)
9. Francesco di Giorgio Martini (1439–1502)
10. Giovanni Duprè (1817–82)

Flowing Lines

The Sienese artists created a proto-Renaissance more graceful and decorative than the strict geometry and naturalism being pursued in Florence. Jacopo della Quercia's tomb of Ilaria *(see also pp42–3)* shows his mastery of sculpting with marble.

Sienese Art

For a short time Siena was as much a centre of artistic innovation as Florence, but sadly it was not destined to play such a big part in the Renaissance. Late 13th-century Sienese art came into its own as painter Duccio and sculptor Jacopo della Quercia started softening and enlivening the prevailing static Byzantine style with Gothic flowing lines and expressive features. By the early 14th century, Simone Martini and the Lorenzetti brothers were adding rich colour palettes and penchant for intricate patterns to the mix. However, whereas Florence's Renaissance went on to revolutionize painting throughout Italy, the idiosyncratic Gothic style of Siena was dealt a crippling blow by the Black Death of 1348. The Lorenzettis died along with two-thirds of the population. A city concerned with rebuilding its economy and fending off Florentine expansion had little time or money for art. By the time Siena got back on its feet, local artists were following a variety of styles, from Gothic to Mannerist.

Tomb of Ilaria del Carretto (1405–6), Jacopo della Quercia

The Maestà (1315), Simone Martini

For more on Siena **See pp86–91**

🔟 Chianti

The 50 km (30 miles) between Florence and Siena is a storybook landscape straight out of a Renaissance painting's background: steeply rolling hills terraced with vineyards and olive groves, crenellated castles and bustling market towns. The seductive beauty of this Tuscan Arcadia has drawn people since Etruscan times; indeed, today it is so popular with the English that it has earned the nickname Chiantishire.

Greve: the main piazza

🅰 A number of local vineyards *(see pp36–7)* host wine tastings with snacks.

You can put together a picnic fit for the gods at butchers such as Falorni in Greve and Prociatti in Radda.

🅒 Call in advance if you plan to visit a vineyard: find out the hours they accept visitors, whether they offer tours (and whether they're free), and ask if you need to make an appointment.

• Map E3 • Tourist Office: Viale G. da Verrazzano 59, Greve in Chianti • 055 854 6287

Chianti Top 10

1. Greve in Chianti
2. Castello di Brolio
3. Radda in Chianti
4. Badia a Passignano
5. Montefioralle
6. Pieve di San Leolino
7. Castellina in Chianti
8. Ipogeo di Montecalvario
9. Badia a Coltibuono
10. Panzano in Chianti

Greve in Chianti

This town has become Chianti's unofficial capital. There are wine shops galore, but the most popular spot is Macelleria Falorni, one of Italy's great butchers, stuffed with hanging *prosciutto*, ageing cheeses and free samples.

Castello di Brolio

A vineyard since 1007, Brolio has been the soul of the Chianti region since "Iron Baron" Bettino Ricasoli, Italy's second prime minister, perfected the Chianti wine formula in the 1800s.

Radda in Chianti

The only hilltop member of the Chianti league (great views) is capped by the 15th-century Palazzo del Podestà studded with stone coats of arms of past mayors. There's another good butcher/grocer's here called Luciano Prociatti.

Montefioralle hamlet

Badia a Passignano

The Antinori wine empire owns the vineyards round this 11th-century monastery. Sunday tours (3pm) get you inside to see Domenico and Davide Ghirlandaio's *Last Supper* fresco and, in the San Michele chapel, baroque paintings by Ridolfo di Ghirlandaio and local boy Il Passignano.

For the top Chianti vineyards See pp36–7

Montefioralle

This 14th-century hamlet, hovering directly above Greve, consists of a single circular street, two churches and fantastic views over the valley and on to the 10th-century Pieve di San Cresci church below the walls.

Pieve di San Leolino

Just south of Panzano lies this little Romanesque church with several Sienese paintings from the 13th to 15th centuries and a pretty little brick cloister.

Ipogeo di Montecalvario

A perfect 6th-century BC tomb, with four passages tunnelling into the burial chambers. There is a light switch beside the gate.

Badia a Coltibuono

This abbey from 770 includes an 11th-century church, Lorenza de' Medici's cookery school and a classy restaurant run by her son Paolo.

Panzano in Chianti

This often-overlooked town (view from town *above*) is the home of Dario Cecchini (arguably Italy's best butcher) and a couple of fine *enoteche*, where you can sample local wines with snacks.

Castellina in Chianti

The most medieval of the Chianti League towns, with a glowering Rocca fortress. Via della Volte – a tunnel-like road pierced by "windows" overlooking the countryside – was a soldiers' walk when this was Florence's last outpost before Siena.

Getting Around

The classic Chianti route is the S222 from Florence to Castellina: either zip straight down to Siena or explore more deeply (highly recommended) by heading east on the S429 through Radda and Gaiole before turning south on the S408 for Siena. But that only takes in the highlights. To truly get a feel for Chianti, explore the back roads to Passignano, Coltibuono and other towns off the beaten path.
Bus services (infrequent!) also connect the main towns.

For more on vineyards and wine See pp62–3

35

Left **Wine tasting** Centre left **Cured hams** Centre right **Ageing in the barrel** Right **Bottled and ready**

Chianti Vineyards

Castello di Brolio
The estate that invented modern Chianti Classico is back in the Ricasoli family's hands. Book tours in advance. ⊗ *Map E4 • 0577 7301*

Monsanto
Wines from an estate that makes a 100 percent Sangiovese Chianti. Call in advance to tour the cellars. ⊗ *Map E3 • 055 805 9000 • www.castellodimonsanto.it*

Fonterutoli
Highly regarded estate in the Marquis Mazzei family since 1435. Excellent Chianti Classico, Badiola Sangioveto and Belguardo (a Morellino). The laid-back bar has tastings. ⊗ *Map E3 • 0577 73 571*

Castello di Ama
You can't tour the estate, but you can taste and buy their Chianti, Merlot and Pinot Grigio at Rinaldi Palmira's enoteca in nearby Lecchi. ⊗ *Map E3*

Castello di Volpaia
Visit the 13th-century village around an impressive central tower, and sample wines, olive oils and vinegars. Call a week in advance to tour. ⊗ *Map E3 • 0577 738 066 • www.volpaia.it*

Castello di Verrazzano
The family has been making wine since 1100. Sample it at the estate on weekdays. ⊗ *Map E3 • 055 854 243 • www.verrazzano.com*

Vicchiomaggio
This dramatically situated and enterprising estate offers tastings, cellar tours (with a day's notice), a trattoria and cooking lessons. ⊗ *Map E3 • 055 854 079 • www.vicchiomaggio.it*

Villa Vignamaggio
A historic villa *(see pp61, 146)* whose wines were the first to be called Chianti. Book ahead for tours. ⊗ *Map E3 • 055 854 661 • www.vignamaggio.com*

Vistarenni
Modern cellars and scenic vineyards, with tastings for small groups who book a day in advance. ⊗ *Map E3 • 0577 738 186*

Rocca delle Macie
A restaurant, rooms to let and an opera festival every summer enliven this estate, with farm buildings dating back to the 14th century. ⊗ *Map E3 • 0577 7321 • www.roccadellemacie.com*

The cellars of Villa Vignamaggio

Top 10 Recent Vintages

1. 1997
2. 1995
3. 1988
4. 1994
5. 1993
6. 1991
7. 1990
8. 1986
9. 1985
10. 1983

Wine Tasting
Most vineyards allow you to sample their wares, and a bottle bought direct from the maker is a wonderful souvenir – or a treat for a picnic. Try not to swallow too much at tastings if you are driving.

The Story of Chianti Classico

Wine from the Classico hills has been enjoyed at least since Roman times (one of its grapes, the Canaiolo, was cultivated by the Etruscans). It's been called Chianti since 1404, when a barrel was sent beyond the area to Prato. A political "Chianti League" of towns was formed in the 13th century, but it took a 1716 grand ducal decree to establish this as the world's first officially defined wine-producing region. In 1960 Chianti became the first Italian "DOCG" – the highest mark of quality. Some 17,400 acres are strung with the grapes – two reds (Sangiovese and Canaiolo) and two whites (Malvasia and Trebbiano) – that make Chianti Classico. Though there are seven Chianti-producing regions, only wines produced in the Classico hills may be called Classico and carry the seal of the Black Cockerel.

The Black Cockerel seal

Top 10 Vineyards

Villa Vignamaggio vineyard

For more on wine **See pp62–3**

37

TOP 10 Cortona

One of Tuscany's most rewarding hill towns, Cortona is a little-known haven of Etruscan tombs, medieval alleyways, Renaissance art, sweeping views and small-town ambience. It was probably settled even before the Etruscans, and later became an important member of that society, as the tombs in its valley attest. Fra Angelico's home, Cortona also gave birth to Renaissance genius Luca Signorelli, Baroque master Pietro da Cortona and 20th-century Futurist Gino Severini.

Piazza Signorelli at the heart of Cortona

🍷 The Enoteria, Via Nazionale 18, offers laid-back wine tastings along with local salumi (cured meats).

🚶 Cortona no longer quite fills its medieval walls. Follow Via S. Margherita as it winds steeply past gardens and Severini-designed shrines to the hilltop Fortezza Medicea for sweeping views over Lake Trasimeno.

• Map F4 • Tourist Office: Via Nazionale 42 • 0575 630 352
• www.cortonaweb.net
• Museo dell'Accademia Etrusca, Nov–Mar: closed Mon; admission charge • Museo Diocesano, closed Mon; admission charge €5
• Melone II del Sodo: no set hours; call to view on 0575 612 565

Top 10 Sights

1. Museo dell'Accademia Etrusca
2. Museo Diocesano
3. Melone II del Sodo
4. Duomo
5. Rugapiana (Via Nazionale)
6. Santa Maria delle Grazie al Calcinaio
7. Melone I del Sodo
8. San Niccolò
9. San Domenico
10. Tomba di Pitagora

Museo dell' Accademia Etrusca

The star piece here is a bronze oil-lamp chandelier depicting figures dancing round Medusa, dated to circa 5th century BC. This is surrounded by ancient bronzes, 15th-century ivories, and paintings by Signorelli, Pinturicchio, Pietro da Cortona and Empoli. There are also small exhibits on Egypt, *objets d'art*, Futurist painter Gino Severini, and the ongoing excavations at the Etruscan site Melone II.

Rugapiana (Via Nazionale)

Museo Diocesano

Small museum housing outstanding works, from a Roman sarcophagus, studied by Donatello, to paintings by Pietro Lorenzetti, Fra Angelico, Luca Signorelli, the studio of Signorelli and his talented nephew Francesco.

Fra Angelico's *Annunciation*, Museo Diocesano

Melone II del Sodo

The remarkable altar on this huge 6th-century BC Etruscan tumulus was discovered in the 1990s. The altar – a sphinx-flanked staircase leading to a wide platform – is orientated towards Cortona up on the hillside, suggesting that this may have been a princely tomb.

For more on Etruscan sights See pp40–41

Duomo
Cortona's barrel-vaulted Renaissance cathedral is filled with decent, but not great, 16th- and 17th-century paintings by Luca Signorelli and others. ✪**3 7 10**

Rugapiana (Via Nazionale)
The main drag of Cortona is the only flat street (*rugapiana* in local dialect) in town. Steep alleyways spill off either side of the pedestrian thoroughfare.

San Niccolò
Tiny 15th-century church beyond a cypress-lined courtyard, housing a Signorelli two-sided altarpiece (ring the bell and ask the custodian to flip it for you).

San Domenico
The church is distinguished by a faded Fra Angelico over the entrance, a Signorelli *Madonna* inside, and a massive, glittering 15th-century altarpiece that is entirely intact (a rarity).

Tomba di Pitagora
The dirt hillock covering this 3rd-century BC tomb was removed long ago. The stone chamber was erroneously dubbed "Pythagoras' Tomb" when somebody confused the mathematician's hometown, Crotone in Calabria, with Cortona.

Cortona Orientation
The road up to the hill town starts near the Melone tombs down on the valley floor. It winds up through olive groves, passing the Tomba di Pitagora and Santa Maria del Calcinaio, before terminating at the bus stop square of Piazza Garibaldi. From here, Via Nazionale leads into the heart of town – piazzas Repubblica and Signorelli – close to most other sights.

Santa Maria delle Grazie al Calcinaio
A set-piece of High Renaissance architecture (1485–1513), the church is the masterpiece of Francesco di Giorgio Martini, set amid olive groves below the town walls.

Melone I del Sodo
The passages of this 6th-century BC Etruscan tomb were shored up in the 19th century. Bookings can be made to get inside to see the remarkable adjoining burial chambers and Etruscan script.

For more hill towns See pp56–7

39

Left **Excavations, Roselle** Centre **Frieze, Chiusi** Right **Tomb, Populonia**

Etruscan Sights Around Cortona

1 Volterra: Museo Etrusco
Etruscans transformed this 9th-century BC town into part of the Dodecapolis confederation. Over 600 marvellous funerary urns fill the museum, which also preserves the *Shade of the Evening* (left), an elegantly elongated bronze boy. (See also p113.)

2 Populonia
Ancient coastal smelting centre *(see p126)*. The medieval town has a small museum and some ancient walls. A nearby necropolis illustrates changing tomb styles, from simple passages to domed tumuli and *edicola* (shrine-type).

3 Sovana: Tombs and Via Cave
Six necropolises surround this Etruscan settlement *(see p126)*, most of them romantically overgrown. The *via cave* are narrow paths carved up to 20 m (65 ft) deep – their function is unknown.

4 Florence: Museo Archeologico
Along with riches from Ancient Rome and Antioch, Florence's oft-overlooked archaeology museum preserves one of the greatest artworks from Etruria, a large, 4th-century BC bronze chimera, probably cast in Chiusi or Orvieto *(see p80)*.

5 Cortona: Museo dell'Accademia Etrusca
Cortona's best museum has a number of superb Etruscan pieces *(see p38)*.

6 Cortona: Tombs
Etruscan tombs in the valley below Cortona include Melone I and II, and the Tomba di Pitagora *(see pp38–9)*.

7 Chiusi: Museo
The once-powerful town of Chiusi attacked Rome in 507 BC. Today, its main museum houses fine jars and funerary urns, some with miraculously preserved polychrome painting *(see p120)*.

8 Chiusi: Tombs
A custodian from Chiusi museum will accompany you to unlock two of the tombs dotting Chiusi's valley, including the Tomba della Pellegrina with its urns and sarcophagi still in place.

9 Grosseto: Museo
Many of the artifacts found in the Maremma (Sovana, Roselle, Vetulonia) made their way here, including terracotta reliefs and painted vases *(see p126)*.

10 Roselle
The only fully excavated Etruscan town in Tuscany. It was once part of Dodecapolis but was conquered early (294 BC). The remains of Etruscan walls and houses lie next to a Roman amphitheatre and baths.

Top 10 Towns Founded by the Etruscans

1 Volterra (Map D4)
2 Arezzo (Map F3)
3 Chiusi (Map F5)
4 Cortona (Map F4)
5 Fiesole (Map E2)
6 Pitigliano (Map F6)
7 Sovana (Map F6)
8 Populonia (Map C5)
9 Saturnia (Map E6)
10 Roselle (Map E5)

Rock-cut tomb, Sovana

The Etruscans

Funerary urn

Tuscany is named after the Etruscans who settled central Italy, from Northern Lazio to the Umbrian Apennines, around the 8th century BC. Little is known about them beyond scant Roman records (the early Roman Tarquin kings were actually Etruscan) and the artifacts that have survived, most of them funerary. They came from Asia Minor (bringing with them Tuscany's familiar cypress tree), enjoyed an advanced culture and relative equality between the sexes, and excelled at engineering – Etruscans taught the Romans the art of draining land for agriculture. They traded extensively with the Greeks, who had settled southern Italy; much Etruscan-era painted pottery is either Greek or Attic-influenced, and the analphabetic Etruscans quickly adopted Greek letters. Their 12 greatest city-states formed a loose, fluctuating confederation called Dodecapolis. By the 3rd century BC, expansion-hungry Romans began conquering Etruria, replacing Etruscan hill towns with Roman valley camps and ruler-straight roads.

Etruscan Cremation Urn

The relief depicts the deceased's last journey into the underworld

Wax writing tablet

Portrait of the deceased

TOP 10 Lucca

Lucca is a genteel city of opera and olive oil, Romanesque churches and hidden palace gardens. Its historic centre is contained within massive 16th-century redbrick bastions. The street plan first laid down by the Romans is little altered – in the Middle Ages the ancient amphitheatre was used as a foundation for houses. Composers Boccherini (1743–1805) and Giacomo Puccini (1858–1924) were born here, and are celebrated in concerts at the 19th-century Teatro del Giglio and in the sumptuous villas north of town.

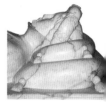
Sculptured soft cushions of the Tomb of Ilaria

Piazza Anfiteatro in Lucca

Top 10 Sights

1. Duomo
2. San Michele in Foro
3. The Walls
4. Tomb of Ilaria
5. Piazza Anfiteatro
6. Museo della San Frediano
7. Torre Guinigi
8. Museo Nazionale di Palazzo Mansi
9. Museo Nazionale Villa Guinigi
10. Santa Maria Forisportam

⊖ Genteel Antico Caffè di Simo, Via Fillungo 58, has catered for everyone from Puccini to Mascagni since 1846.

⊘ Lucchesi are cyclists; there are several rental outfits on Piazza Santa Maria.

• Tourist Office: Piazza Santa Maria 35, Telephone 0583 91 991 www.luccaturismo.it
• Duomo open daily; admission charge for Tomb of Ilaria • San Frediano open daily
• Torre Guinigi open daily; admission charge
• Museo Nazionale di Palazzo Mansi closed Mon; admission charge
• Museo Nazionale Guinigi closed Mon; admission charge; combined ticket also allows access to both museums

Duomo
The early 13th-century façade stacks Pisan-Romanesque arcades over a portico of Romanesque carvings. Inside are sculptures by 15th-century master Matteo Civitale, Ilaria's tomb *(top)*, Tintoretto's *Last Supper* (1591), and the revered *Volto Santo*, supposedly carved by Nicodemus.

San Michele in Foro
Built atop the Roman Forum, San Michele's striking Pisan-Romanesque arcades are stacked even higher than the Duomo's. Inside are a *Madonna and Child* by Civitale, another by Andrea della Robbia, and a Filippo Lippi *Saints*. Composer Puccini was a chorister here.

The Walls
Chestnuts and umbrella pines shade the gravelly path atop Lucca's remarkable ramparts (1544-1650). Locals love to stroll or bicycle this circuit for views down into palazzo gardens and out over the Apuan Alps.

Tomb of Ilaria

Jacopo della Quercia's masterpiece (1405–7) in the Sacristy of the Duomo marries the medieval lying-in-state pose of town boss Paolo Guinigi's young wife (she died at 26) with classical-inspired garlands and cherubs. Jacopo's delicate chisel turned hard marble into soft cushions *(left)* and captured Ilaria's ethereal beauty.

Torre Guinigi

The 14th-century palace of Lucca's ruling family sprouts a 44-m (144-ft) tower, with stunning panoramas.

Museo Nazionale Guinigi

This 15th-century villa houses a fine archaeology section of Iron Age, Ligurian and later Etruscan finds, decent Renaissance paintings, and 15th-century wood inlay.

Santa Maria Forisportam

Though the Pisan façade is 12th century, the interior is mostly 17th century, including two Guercino altarpieces and a *pietre dure* ciborium (inlaid stone vessel).

Lucca's History

Villa Guinigi's collections show the region's Stone Age history, but the town was founded by the Romans. Caesar, Pompey and Crassus made their First Triumverate here. St Peter's disciple Paulinus legendarily brought Christianity to Lucca, and it was a way-station on the Francigena pilgrimage route. Strongwoman Marquesa Mathilda ruled during the Lombard period. Succeeded by local lords (save during a 14th-century stint under Pisa), Lucca remained proudly autonomous of Florence's Grand Duchy until Napoléon gave the city to his sister Elisa in 1805.

Piazza Anfiteatro

Lucca's Roman amphitheatre was long ago mined for building stone, but its oval remained as a base for medieval houses. It's now a quiet piazza, with ancient arches embedded in house walls.

Museo Nazionale di Palazzo Mansi

Riotous baroque palace interiors serve as a backdrop for Renaissance and Mannerist paintings by Pontormo, Bronzino, Beccafumi, Correggio, Sodoma and Luca Giordano.

Museo della San Frediano

The façade glitters with Byzantine mosaics *(right)*. Among its treasures are a carved Romanesque font and Amico Aspertini's quirky fresco cycle (1508–9), the *Miracles of San Frediano*.

Left **Duomo Campanile** Centre **San Miniato al Monte** Right **Santissima Annunziata**

🔟 Churches in Florence

Santa Croce, façade

1 Duomo
See pp12–13.

2 Santa Croce
Gothic pantheon of cultural heroes, containing the tombs of Michelangelo, Machiavelli, Rossini and Galileo (reburied here in 1737). Giotto frescoed the two chapels to the right of the altar. ◉ *Piazza S Croce • Map P4–5 • Open 9:30am–5:30pm Mon–Sat, 1–5:30pm Sun • Admission charge includes museum ticket*

3 Santa Maria Novella
Among the master-pieces here are Masaccio's *Trinità* (1428; painting's first use of perspective), Giotto's *Crucifix*, Filippino Lippi's *Cappella Strozzi* frescoes (1486) and Ghirlandaio's decorous

Interior, Santa Maria Novella

sanctuary frescoes (1485). The cloisters' greenish Noah frescoes (1446) are warped perspectives by Paolo Uccello. ◉ *Piazza S Maria Novella • Map L2 • Open 9am–5pm Mon–Thu, Sat, 9am–2pm Sun • Closed Fri • Admission charge*

4 San Lorenzo and the Medici Chapels
San Lorenzo was the Medici parish church. The family tombs are decorated by Donatello, Rosso Fiorentino, Bronzino and Filippo Lippi, with architecture by Brunelleschi (interior and Old Sacristy) and Michelangelo (Laurentian Library and New Sacristy). The New Sacristy contains Michelangelo's roughly finished *Dawn, Dusk, Day* and *Night*. ◉ *Piazza di S Lorenzo • Map M2 • Basilica: open 10am–5pm Mon–Sat, Medici Chapel: open 8:15am–5pm daily (to 1:50pm Sun; closed 1st and 3rd Mon of month) • Admission charge*

5 Santo Spirito
Brunelleschi's masterpiece of Renaissance design. The building's proportions are picked out in clean lines of *pietra serena* stone against white plaster. Seek out altarpieces by Filippino Lippi (*Madonna and Child with Saints*, 1466) and Verrocchio (a minimalist *St Monica and Augustinian Nuns*). ◉ *Piazza S Spirito • Map L5 • Open 8:30am–noon, 4–6:30pm Mon–Sat, 4–6:30pm Sun • Free*

For great churches outside Florence **See pp46–7**

6 Santa Maria del Carmine

Masolino started the Brancacci Chapel's frescoes of St Peter's life in 1424. Another of his works, *Adam and Eve*, is rather sweet compared to the powerful *Expulsion from the Garden* by his successor, Masaccio. Filippino Lippi completed the cycle in 1485. ⊗ *Piazza del Carmine • Map K4 • Open 10am–5pm Mon–Sat, 1pm–5pm Sun • Admission charge for Brancacci Chapel*

7 San Miniato al Monte

This is Florence's only Romanesque church, its green and white façade perched high above the city. The doors of Michelozzo's tabernacle were painted by Agnolo Gaddi (1394–6). ⊗ *Via Monte alle Croci • Map E3 • Open 8am–12:30pm, 2:30–7:30pm Mon–Sat, 3–6pm Sun (summer: 8am–7:30pm daily) • Free*

8 Orsanmichele

Granary-turned-church ringed with statues by Donatello, Ghiberti and Verrocchio (copies; the originals are in an upstairs museum). Orcagna designed the tabernacle to resemble a miniature cathedral containing a *Madonna and Child* (1348) by Bernardo Daddi. ⊗ *Via dell'Arte della Lana • Map M4 • Open 9am–noon, 4–6pm daily • Closed first & last Mon of month • Admission charge for museum*

Michelangelo's funerary figures, the Medici Chapel

9 Santa Trinità

Buontalenti provided the façade, while Ghirlandaio frescoed the Cappella

Colonnaded aisle, Santo Spirito

Sasetti with the *Life of St Francis* set in 15th-century Florence. ⊗ *Piazza S Trinità • Map L4 • Open 8am–noon, 4–6pm Mon–Sat, 4–6pm Sun • Free*

10 Santissima Annunziata

The Michelozzo-designed entry cloister was frescoed by Mannerists Andrea del Sarto, Rosso and Pontormo. The Baroque, octagonal tribune is decorated with Perugino's *Madonna and Saints* and Bronzino's *Resurrection*. Sculptures by Giambologna festoon his tomb in the back chapel. ⊗ *Piazza SS Annunziata • Map P1 • Open 7:30am–12:30pm, 4–6:30pm • Free*

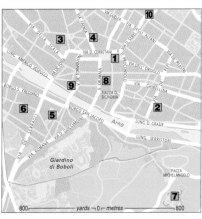

For more on Florence **See pp76–83**

Left **Siena's Duomo** Centre **Duomo, Pisa** Right **Sant'Antimo**

🔟 Churches Outside Florence

1 Siena's Duomo
A striped Romanesque-Gothic pile, richly decorated by the likes of Giovanni Pisano, Donatello, Pinturicchio, Michelangelo, Beccafumi and Bernini *(see pp26–7)*.

Ceiling of the Collegiata, San Gimignano

2 San Gimignano's Collegiata
The "Medieval Manhattan's" main church is covered inside with 14th- and 15th-century frescoes, including a cycle by Ghirlandaio in the Chapel of St Fina. *(See also p18.)* ◈ Map D3 • Piazza del Duomo • 9:30am–7:10pm Mon–Fri (to 5pm Nov–Mar), 9:30am–5pm Sat, 1–5pm Sun • Closed during religious services; 27 Jan–28 Feb • Admission charge

3 Pisa's Duomo
Beside the Pisan-Romanesque exterior, only a few elements, such as Cimabue's apse mosaic of 1302, survived a 1595 fire. However, the late Renaissance/early Baroque refurbishment was stylish, and local legend holds the swinging of the nave's large bronze lamp inspired Galileo's Law of Pendulums. *(See also p18.)*

4 Lucca's Duomo
San Martino is a masterpiece of Romanesque stacked open arcades, stuffed with sculpture from Gothic reliefs to works by two great 15th-century talents, local Matteo Civitale and Sienese Jacopo della Quercia. *(See also pp42–3.)* ◈ Map C2 • Piazza San Martino • Open 9am–7pm • Free

5 Sant'Antimo
This isolated Cistercian abbey was founded by Charlemagne, but the building dates from 1118. Inside, several column capitals are beautifully carved in alabaster. White-robed monks sing a Gregorian chant five times daily; ask them for a peek at the sacristy's earthy frescoes. *(See also p119.)* ◈ Map E5 • Abbazia di Sant' Antimo • Open 10:30am–12:30pm, 3–6:30pm Mon–Sat; 9:15–10:45am, 3–6pm Sun • Free

Cattedrale di San Martino, Lucca

For the great churches of Florence **See pp44–5**

Duomo, Massa Marittima

Massa Marittima's Duomo

6 A split personality cathedral: Romanesque arcading topped by Gothic pinnacles and belltower. It houses wonderfully idiosyncratic sculpture: three takes on the life of local patron San Cerbone and lovely pre-Romanesque carvings. ⓢ *Map D4/5 • Piazza Garibaldi • Open 8am-noon, 3-6pm • Free*

Prato's Duomo

7 Michelozzo's outside pulpit ensures that crowds in the piazza are able to see the bishop display the Virgin's girdle *(see p29)*. The graceful frescoes in the choir by Filippo Lippi include a famous scene of Salomé presenting Herod with the head of John the Baptist on a platter. ⓢ *Map D2 • Piazza Duomo • Open 7am-noon, 3:30-7pm Mon-Sat; 7am-1pm, 3:30-8pm Sun • Free*

Arezzo's San Francesco

8 A 15-year restoration of the choir's *Legend of the True Cross* (1448-66), the greatest fresco cycle by Piero della Francesca, has revived the vitality and vibrancy of this masterpiece. ⓢ *Map F3 • Piazza S Francesco • Open 9am-7pm Mon-Fri; 9am-6:15pm Sat; 1-6:15pm Sun (to 5:45pm Sat-Sun in winter) • Advance booking required (063 2810 or www.pierodella francesca.it) • Admission charge for Piero frescoes*

Pistoia's Duomo

9 Andrea della Robbia's enamelled terracotta entrance accents the Romanesque exterior's zebra stripes. The Altar of St Jacobo (1287-1456) contains some of Italy's finest silversmithing. Ask the custodian to show you Verrocchio's *Madonna di Piazza* (1485). ⓢ *Map D2 • Piazza del Duomo • Open 8:30am-12:30pm, 3:30-7pm • Admission charge for St Jacobo's chapel*

Pienza's Duomo

10 Behind the Classical façade is a reinterpreted German Gothic building, the result of Piccolomini Pope Pius II's interference in Rossellino's initial plan to build the perfect Renaissance town. ⓢ *Map F4 • Piazza Pio II • Open 7am-1pm, 2:30-7pm • Free*

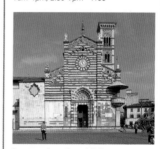

Duomo and exterior pulpit, Prato

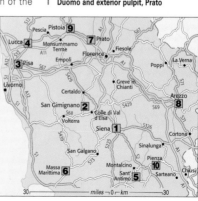

Left **Boboli Gardens, Pitti Palace** Centre **Museo dell'Accademia Etrusco** Right **Pitti Palace**

🔟 Museums

1 Florence's Uffizi
Botticelli's *Birth of Venus*, Leonardo's *Annunciation* and Michelangelo's *Holy Family* are just three of the masterpieces that make this the top sight in all of Tuscany *(see pp8–11)*.

2 Florence's Pitti Palace
The Galleria Palatina features Raphael Madonnas and Titian beauties alongside works by Andrea del Sarto, Perugino, Signorelli, Caravaggio and Rubens. Palatial décor is the backdrop to collections of costumes, silverware and carriages *(see pp14–17)*.

3 Siena's Museo Civico
A battlemented medieval town hall with the best Gothic painting in Siena *(see p32)*, including Lorenzetti's incomparable *Allegory of Good and Bad Government*.

4 Florence's Bargello
Italy's top sculpture gallery, with the world's best collection of Donatellos *(right)*. Other sculptures by Cellini, Giambologna and Michelangelo.
⊛ *Via del Proconsolo 4 • Map N4 • Open 8:15am– 2pm daily • Closed 2nd and 4th Mon, and 1st, 3rd and 5th Sun of month • Admission charge*

5 Volterra's Museo Etrusco Guarnacci
One of Tuscany's top Etruscan museums. Over 600 marble and alabaster funerary urns carved with myths or metaphors for the afterlife, a terracotta sarcophagus lid of an elderly couple, and small bronzes including the elongated boyish figure, *Shade of the Evening*. ⊛ *Via Don Minzoni 15 • Map D4 • Open 9am–7pm daily (to 1:45pm Nov–Mar) • Admission charge*

6 Florence's Accademia
The crowds come for Michelangelo's *David* (1501–4), then stay for his *Slaves*, carved for the tomb of Julius II, and paintings by Botticelli, Lorenzo di Credi, Orcagna, Perugino and del Sarto. ⊛ *Via Ricasoli 60 • Map N1 • Open 8:15am–6:50pm Tue–Sun, occasional extended hours in summer • Admission charge*

7 Sansepolcro's Museo Civico
Piero della Francesca's home town retained some of his greatest, most psychologically penetrating works, including *Madonna della Misericordia* (1445–62), *San Giuliano* (1458) and the eerie *Resurrection* (1463), called the "best picture of the world" by Aldous Huxley.
⊛ *Via Aggiunti 65 • Map F3 • Open 9am– 1:30pm, 2:30–7:30pm daily Jun–Sep; 9:30am–1pm, 2:30–6pm Oct–May • Admission charge*

The Resurrection (1463) in Sansepolcro's Museo Civico

Siena's Pinacoteca Nazionale

It may lack towering masterpieces, but this is Tuscany's best survey of Sienese painting. ◈ *Via S. Pietro 29 • Map E4 • Open 8am–7pm Tue–Sat, 8am–1:30pm Sun–Mon • Admission charge*

Cortona's Museo dell'Accademia Etrusca

This hotchpotch collection preserves Etruscan finds as well as Renaissance and Baroque paintings, a few Egyptian artifacts, decorative arts, and works by the local Futurist Gino Severini. ◈ *Piazza Signorelli • Map F4 • Open 10am–7pm Tue–Sun (to 5pm Oct–Mar) • Admission charge*

Florence's Science Museum

The instruments displayed here are often as beautiful as they are scientifically significant. Exhibits include a mechanical "calculator" made of engraved disks, a perpetual motion machine and the telescopes with which Galileo discovered the moons of Jupiter. ◈ *Piazza dei Giudici 1 • Map N5 • Open 9:30am–5pm Mon, Wed–Sat, 9:30am–1pm Tue. Also open 2nd Sun of month, 10am–1pm • Admission charge*

Artistic Styles

Etruscan
Heavily influenced by Greek art. Funerary urns and large statues and bronze votives of the 8th–4th centuries BC.

Byzantine
Conservative, static, stylized in Eastern iconographic tradition of the 9th–13th centuries AD. Almond faces, large eyes, robes pleated in gold cross-hatching.

Gothic
More expressive, colourful and realistic than Byzantine. Flowing lines and dramatic gestures (13th–14th centuries).

Renaissance
Tuscany's greatest contribution to art history. In their elegant compositions, the 15th- and 16th-century Florentine artists developed a more naturalistic style and techniques such as perspective.

Mannerism
Late Renaissance, 16th-century offshoot based on the twisting poses and rich colour palette of Michelangelo.

Baroque
Similar to Mannerism, but using strong contrasts of light and shade to achieve high drama (16th–17th centuries).

Rococo
Baroque gone chaotic, effusive and overwrought (18th century).

Neoclassical
Based on Classical models and mythological themes (19th century).

Macchiaioli
Tuscan cousin of Impressionism (late 19th century).

Liberty
Italian 20th-century Art Nouveau, seen mostly on façades and shop signs.

For more on artists **See pp50–1**

Left *The Death of St Francis,* Giotto Right *Self Portrait,* Raphael

🔟 Tuscan Artists

Self-Portrait, Leonardo da Vinci

1 Giotto (1266–1337)
A shepherd boy who dragged painting from its static, Byzantine methodology and set it on the road to the Renaissance. He imbued his paintings with earthy reality, giving his figures bulk and expressiveness.

2 Simone Martini (1284–1344)
Martini took a medieval eye for narrative and iconography and married it to a vibrant Gothic palette, richly patterned fabrics and intense drama in his courtly, graceful figures.

3 Donatello (1386–1466)
The first fully Renaissance sculptor worked out perspective in sculpture well before painters got there. He cast the first free-standing nude and first equestrian statue since antiquity, and came up with the *schiacciato* technique, using etched perspective lines to create the illusion of great depth in a shallow relief.

4 Fra Angelico (1395–1455)
A devout Dominican friar, Beato (Italians honour him as beatified) Angelico's origins as a manuscript illuminator informed his art. But his work is grounded in the Renaissance precepts of naturalism and perspective.

5 Masaccio (1401–1428)
Not only did Masaccio imbue Renaissance painting with an unflinching naturalism, he also perfected single point perspective (Florence's Santa Maria Novella's *Trinità*). Not the best draughtsman, but his strong brushstrokes and penetrating scenes are a cornerstone of Renaissance art.

6 Piero della Francesca (1416–92)
A visionary early Renaissance master whose paintings have an ethereal spirituality, his well-modelled figures endowed with great humanity. His complex compositions also show his early mastery of perspective.

7 Botticelli (1444–1510)
Renaissance master of languid figures populating grand mythological scenes. He got caught up in Florence's spiritual crisis, and is said to have tossed his own "blasphemous" canvases upon Savonarola's "Bonfires

For more on Tuscany's masterpieces **See pp52–3**

of the Vanities" *(see p78)*. He spent the rest of his career painting vapid Madonnas and uninspired religious scenes.

8 Leonardo da Vinci
(1452–1519)

The ultimate Renaissance Man: a genius painter, inventor and proto-scientist, with a penchant for experimentation but a short attention span (he left much unfinished). His *sfumato* technique of blurring outlines and hazy backgrounds lent his works tremendous depth and realism.

9 Michelangelo (1475–1564)

Famously irascible, he was a sculptor of genius by his early 20s, who only painted the Sistine Chapel under protest. He also found time to design Florence's defences, write quality sonnets and become a significant architect.

10 Pontormo (1494–1556)

Mixing Andrea del Sarto's experimentation with twisting figures and Michelangelo's use of non-primary colours, Pontormo took these concepts to vivid and complex extremes.

The Visitation, Pontormo

Other Artists in Tuscany

1 Giovanni Bellini
(1435–1516)
Teacher of Giorgione and Titian, noted for his early use of oils and fluid style.

2 Perugino (1446–1523)
Probably studied in Florence, possibly alongside Leonardo. Taught Raphael and Pinturicchio.

3 Pinturicchio (1454–1513)
Added Tuscan humanism to Umbrian Renaissance style.

4 Giorgione (1478–1510)
Early Venetian master whose use of dark oils came from Leonardo. A great influence on the young Titian.

5 Titian (1480–1576)
Greatest Venetian painter. Paintings such as his *Venus of Urbino* hang in the Uffizi *(see p9)*.

6 Raphael (1483–1520)
Took Perugino's Umbrian style, and mixed it with Leonardo's techniques and Michelangelo's innovations to become supreme.

7 Tintoretto (1519–94)
Aspiring to the grace of Michelangelo, Tintoretto worked with a more sombre palette than that used by Titian.

8 Giambologna
(1529–1608)
Greatest Mannerist sculptor. Broke with tradition to create statues that require 360-degree viewing to appreciate.

9 Caravaggio (1571–1609)
Roman Baroque master whose life came to an untimely close in Tuscany.

10 Rubens (1577–1640)
Early Baroque Flemish master who adapted Italian style to Northern tastes.

 For Florence's top art collections **See pp8–17**

Left **Pisa's Duomo Group** Right **Panels from the *Gates of Paradise*, Baptistry, Florence**

🔟 Tuscan Masterpieces

David
At the age of 26, Michelangelo took on a huge slab of marble, nicknamed "the Giant" by the sculptors of the day, and turned it into *David* (1501–4, *above*), an intense young man contemplating his task as a proper Renaissance humanist would. Intended for Florence's Duomo, it first stood in front of the Palazzo Vecchio, was damaged during an anti-Medici riot, and eventually wheeled to the Accademia for safekeeping. ⑤ *Florence, Accademia* (see p77)

Birth of Venus
Botticelli's beauty strikes a Classical, modest pose, covering her nakedness with her hands while an Hour rushes to clothe her and the west wind, Zephyr, blows her gracefully to shore in a swirl of pink roses (1485). ⑤ *Florence, Uffizi* (see p8)

Leonardo's Annunciation
One of Leonardo da Vinci's first paintings, produced between 1472 and 1475 apparently while still a student in Verrocchio's workshop. It displays his early mastery of *sfumato* technique and Renaissance penchant for the Classical. ⑤ *Florence, Uffizi* (see p8)

Gates of Paradise
It took Ghiberti many years (1425–52) to complete 10 gilded bronze panels of Old Testament scenes on the Baptistry's east doors (now copies; originals in the Museo dell'Opera).
⑤ *Florence, Baptistry* (see p12)

Trinità
Masaccio's *Trinità* is the first painting to use mathematical single point perspective (1428). The triangular composition draws lines from the kneeling donors through the halos of Mary and St John to God the Father. ⑤ *Florence, Santa Maria Novella* (see p44)

Giotto's Maestà
Giotto's masterful altarpiece (1310) broke conventions by dressing the Virgin in normal

Birth of Venus by Botticelli

For more about the Uffizi masterpieces See pp8–11

The Annunciation, San Marco, Florence

clothes rather than stylized robes, with the Child perched on an actual lap rather than hovering.
Ⓝ *Florence, Uffizi (see p9)*

Fra Angelico's Annunciation
This version of the Annunciation was painted in 1442 by Fra Angelico for his own monastery. The sense of space is emphasized by showing the room behind the loggia, and the lush woods in the distance beyond.
Ⓝ *Florence, San Marco (see p78)*

Duccio's Maestà
The first undisputed masterpiece of the Sienese School was this *Maestà* (1311) by Duccio. It was paraded through the streets, and painting a *Maestà* became a rite of passage for Sienese artists.
Ⓝ *Siena, Museo Metropolitana (see p28)*

Allegory of Good and Bad Government
Ambrogio Lorenzetti's fresco of 1338 wraps around the medieval ruling Council of Nine's inner chamber. Ruled by the allegorical figures of Good Government, medieval Siena prospers. Under Bad Government, it crumbles.
Ⓝ *Siena, Museo Civico (see pp30 & 32)*

Resurrection of Christ
As Piero della Francesca's heavy-lidded, heavily muscled Jesus rises from his sarcophagus, the dreary, dead landscape flowers into life (1463). The sleeping Roman soldier slumped in brown armour is said to be a self-portrait.
Ⓝ *Sansepolcro, Museo Civico (see p101)*

Top 10 Architectural Highlights

1 The Dome of Florence's Duomo
Brunelleschi's ingenious double-shell dome revived the genius of ancient builders to kick-start Renaissance architecture (see pp12–13).

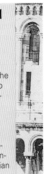

2 Florence's Santa Maria Novella
Alberti's mathematically precise Renaissance façade contrasts with the textbook Italian Gothic interior (see p44).

3 Florence's Palazzo Vecchio
Arnolfo di Cambio's asymmetrical masterpiece of Gothic civic architecture (see p78).

4 Florence's Santo Spirito
Brunelleschi's perfectly proportioned interior set the Renaissance standard (see p44).

5 Pisa's Duomo Group
Beautiful assemblage of Pisan-Romanesque buildings using grey-and-white marble bands, blind arcades, and stacked loggias (see pp22–3).

6 Pisa's Santa Maria della Spina
Jewel of a Gothic church: all pointy arches, spires and statuettes (see p24).

7 Montepulciano's Tempio di San Biagio
High Renaissance masterpiece of proportion (see p119).

8 Pienza's Piazza Pio II
Perfectly planned Renaissance town centre (see p119).

9 Sant'Antimo
Gorgeous French-style Romanesque Cistercian abbey in the countryside (see p46).

10 San Gimignano
Best-preserved medieval hill town, complete with 14 stone towers (see pp18–19).

For more on the great Tuscan churches **See pp44–7**

Left **Medici coat of arms** Centre **San Marco, built by Cosimo il Vecchio** Right **Cosimo I**

🔟 Medici Rulers

Lorenzo the Magnificent

1 Giovanni de' Bicci
(1360–1429)

Founded the Medici fortune by making his family's bank the bank for the papal Curia. He also served as head of the *priori* government and was a sponsor of Ghiberti's Baptistry commission.

2 Cosimo il Vecchio
(1389–1464)

Adroitly managed his family fortune, political clout and personal image to become the *de facto* ruler of Florence. Each time he was exiled or imprisoned by rivals, popular sentiment brought him back to power.

3 Lorenzo the Magnificent
(1449–92)

Most beloved of the Medici. A devout humanist and patron of the arts (and a fair poet himself) who, alongside many accomplishments of his own, sponsored Michelangelo's early career. Able ruler of the city.

4 Pope Leo X
(Giovanni; 1475–1521)

Lorenzo the Magnificent's son continued to call the shots from Rome, exclaiming "God has risen us to the papacy; let us enjoy it." The younger brother and nephews he groomed to take over Florence all died, and so his cousin, Cardinal Giulio, took the reins.

5 Pope Clement VII
(Giulio; 1478–1534)

Cardinal Giulio fared well when running Florence himself, but once he became Pope spent his energies fighting Emperor Charles V, leaving Florence in the hands of his incompetent young relatives Alessandro and Ippolito.

6 Alessandro (1511–37)

Clement VII's bastard son inherited the ducal mantle at 19, and soon became a despot,

Pope Leo X

For more on the artists patronized by the Medici See pp50–51

carousing with his cousin Lorenzino, who eventually grew jealous and murdered Alessandro.

Ferdinando I

7 Cosimo I (1519–74)
The first Medici to gain the title grand duke was created Duke at the age of 17, when the first primary Medici line petered out. He conquered Siena, built a port (Livorno) and ruled judiciously but with something of an iron fist.

8 Ferdinando I (1549–1609)
Popular, hands-on grand duke who founded hospitals, gave poor girls dowries, promoted agriculture and hosted grand parties. He married Christine of Lorraine, whose family would inherit the grand ducal title.

9 Anna Maria (1667–1743)
The last of the main Medici line. She willed all Medici possessions – including the collections in the Uffizi, Pitti and Bargello – to the Lorraine grand dukes on the stipulation the patrimony could never be removed from Florence.

10 Gian Gastone (1671–1737)
The last Medici ruler was an obese sensualist who rarely stirred from bed, where he frequently cavorted with nubile young men. Occasionally he ventured forth to prove he was alive, guzzling wine inside his carriage and leaning out only to vomit on his subjects. Unsurprisingly, his death was unmourned, and with his demise the Grand Ducal title passed to the Austrian Lorraines.

Medici Support for the Arts

1 Michelangelo
Lorenzo the Magnificent recruited the young artist to study the sculptures in the Medici gardens.

2 Donatello
Cosimo il Vecchio's will saw that the sculptor never lacked for commissions; Donatello is buried near Cosimo in San Lorenzo.

3 Galileo
Cosimo II protected the iconoclastic scientist from the Inquisition, bargaining his death sentence down to excommunication and house arrest.

4 Uffizi
Francesco I opened this gallery of the family's art collections on the third floor of their offices (see pp8–9).

5 Botticelli
A Medici cousin commissioned the *Birth of Venus* and *Primavera* for his villa.

6 Pitti Palace
The Grand Ducal home has many works from the Medici's collections (see pp14–17).

7 San Marco
Cosimo il Vecchio built the monastery, including Europe's first public library (see p78).

8 World's First Opera
Ferdinando I commissioned *Dafne*, a story set to music, from Jacopo Peri and Ottavio Rinuccini for his wedding (1589).

9 Benvenuto Cellini
Cosimo I convinced Cellini to return to Florence to make his masterpiece, *Perseus*.

10 Opificio delle Pietre Dure
Ferdinando I founded this inlaid stone workshop, also Florence's chief laboratory for art restoration.

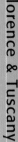

BENVENUTO CELLINI
MAESTRO
GLI ORAFI
DI FIRENZE

For more on Medici palaces and villas **See pp14–17 & 60–61**

Left **Piazza, Pienza** Centre **Image in Volterra's Duomo** Right **Volterra**

10 Hill Towns

Siena
1 Siena may have grown to small city size, but it retains a homey, hill-town atmosphere. Its travertine-accented brick palaces, stone towers and fabulously decorated churches are strung along three high ridges at the south end of the Chianti hills. *(See pp26–9 & 86–91.)* Map E4

San Gimignano
2 The epitome of the perfect Italian hill town. The pride of this "Medieval Manhattan" is a group of 14 stone towers that seemingly sprout from the terracotta roof tiles. San Gimignano is surrounded by patchwork fields and vineyards producing Tuscany's best DOCG white wine. *(See pp18–19.)* Map D3

Medieval tower, Cortona

Volterra
3 The world's greatest alabaster craftsmen inhabit the loftiest hill town in Tuscany, whose stony medieval streets rise a cloud-scraping 555 m (1,820 ft) above the valley. This was one of the key cities in the Etruscan Dodecapolis confederation *(see pp40–41)*. The museum *(see p48)* is filled with finds unearthed as the erosion that is affecting one end of town slowly exposes ancient tombs. Map D4

Montepulciano
4 The town rises from a Medici city gate to the hilltop Piazza Grande with its crenellated Michelozzo-designed Palazzo Comunale and brick-façaded Duomo. Along the way, the main street passes Renaissance palaces, 19th-century cafés and dozens of wine shops where the samples of *grappa* and Vino Nobile *(see pp62–3)* flow freely. You can also visit the cellars beneath the town. Map F4

Cortona
5 This Etruscan settlement above the Chiana Valley is a trove of ancient tombs and Renaissance art. Stony buildings, steep streets and interlocked *piazze* characterize the centre. The upper half of Cortona has a sanctuary, the 16th-century Medici fortress, numerous gardens and little-known lookouts. *(See pp38–41.)* Map F4

6 Montalcino

Montalcino stands proudly high above the valley; this was the last ally of Siena against Florentine rule. The hilltop eyrie is dominated by the

The clifftop town of Pitigliano

shell of a 14th-century fortress, which has fantastic views, and is now a place where you can sample Montalcino's Brunello wine *(see pp62–3)*, Tuscany's most robust red. ◈ *Map E4*

7 Pienza

Italy's only perfectly planned Renaissance town centre was commissioned from Rossellino by Pope Pius II. The perimeter street offers views over the rumpled green, sheep-dotted landscape. The town's many little shops specialize in Tuscan wines, honey and the best *pecorino* sheep's milk cheese in all of Italy. ◈ *Map F4*

8 Massa Marittima

Two hill towns in one. The "Old Town" centres on a triangular piazza with the Duomo and the crenellated mayor's *palazzo* (a museum of local antiquities and Ambrogio Lorenzetti's *Maestà*). The upper "New Town" was founded in the 14th century by

the conquering Sienese. Their fortress offers sweeping views over the hills. ◈ *Map D4/5*

9 Pitigliano

In the heart of the Etruscan Maremma, surrounded by valleys full of ancient tombs, Pitigliano is built upon an outcrop of tufa rock. In fact, it is difficult to tell where the cliff sides end – pockmarked as they are with cellar windows – and the walls of the houses and castle begin. ◈ *Map F6*

10 Fiesole

Fiesole was the hilltop town that Roman Fiorentina was built to compete with. The town has a Roman theatre, small museums of art and archaeology, cool summertime breezes and views across to Florence. ◈ *Map E2*

Massa Marittima

Following pages **Duomo, Prato**

Left **Wine tasting, Villa Vignamaggio** Right **Villa di Artimino "La Ferdinanda"**

🔟 Villas and Gardens

Villa Poggio a Caiano
Giuliano da Sangallo restructured (1480) this greatest Medici villa for Lorenzo the Magnificent. The ballroom is a pinnacle of Mannerist painting by Pontormo, Andrea del Sarto and Alessandro Allori. Francesco I and his second wife Bianca Cappello died here in 1587, apparently poisoned. 🞄 *Piazza de' Medicea 14 • Map D2 • 055 877 012 • Open Nov–Feb: 8:30am–3:30pm; Mar & Oct: 8:15am–4:30pm; Apr, May, Sep: 8:15am–5:30pm; Jun & Aug: 8:15am–6:30pm (ticket office closes 1 hour before) • Admission charge*

Villa Demidoff
Buontalenti laid out the vast Pratolino park for Francesco I de' Medici (1568–81). The waterworks of luminous jet sprays and singing fountains have long fallen into disrepair (the villa was demolished in 1824), but what remains is still spectacular, especially the figure of Appennino rising out of a lily pond. 🞄 *Pratolino • Map E2 • 055 409 427 • Open Apr–Sep: 10am–8:30pm Thu–Sun; Mar: 10am–6pm Sun • Admission charge*

Appennino rising out of a lily pond, Villa Demidoff

Villa della Petraia
This villa was rebuilt for Ferdinando I de' Medici by Buontalenti (1595). Volterrano decorated the courtyard with the *Glory of the Medici* frescoes (1636–48). The English-style park is 17th-century. 🞄 *Via della Petraia 40 • Map E2 • 055 452 691 • Open Nov–Feb: 8:15am–4:30pm; Mar, Oct: 8:15am–5:30pm; Apr, May, Sep: 8:15am–6:30pm; Jun, Jul: 8:15am–7:30pm • Closed 2nd & 3rd Mon of month • Admission charge*

Villa Reale di Marlia
This 16th-century villa was radically altered by Elisa Baciocchi to suit her 19th-century Napoleonic tastes. Only the 17th-century gardens are open. 🞄 *Marlia, Capannori • Map D2 • 0583 30 009 • Open Mar–Nov: hourly tours 10am–1pm, 2–5pm • Closed Mon • Admission charge*

Painting of the Poggio A Caiano by Giusto Utens

For more about the Medici family See pp54–5

Villa Mansi

The 16th-century statue-studded villa contains mythological frescoes painted in the late 18th century. Juvarra's Baroque gardens survive to the west side of the villa; the rest were landscaped in English style in the 19th century. ◈ *Segromigno in Monte • Map D2 • Open 9am–1pm, 3:30–8pm Tue–Sat (to 5pm in winter) • Admission charge*

Villa di Artimino "La Ferdinanda"

A 16th-century Buontalenti villa for Ferdinando I. The multitude of chimneys and lack of gardens hint that this was a hunting lodge for winter sport. The basement houses a small museum of archaeology. ◈ *Artimino, Carmignano • Map D2 • House open by appointment (055 875 1427) • Free*

Villa Garzoni

Though the villa (1633–52) is currently closed, the 17th- and 18th-century park, which is set into a steep hillside with statues and fountains aplenty, is still open to the public. ◈ *Collodi • Map D2 • Open 9am–sunset • Admission charge*

Villa di Castello

Cosimo I had Tribolo lay out the marvellous gardens in 1541, a combination of clipped hedges, ponds, ilex woods and statuary. Only the gardens are open.

Villa Vignamaggio

◈ *Via di Castello 47, Sesto Fiorentino • Map E2 • Open Sep–May: 9am–sunset; Jun–Aug: 8:15–sunset • Closed 2nd & 3rd Mon of month • Admission charge*

Villa Vignamaggio

The villa's wines were the first to be called "Chianti" (in 1404). This is also where the real Mona Lisa was born (1479) and where, more recently, *Much Ado about Nothing* was filmed. Guided tours include wine samples; a full tour includes lunch. ◈ *Vignamaggio, Greve • Map E3 • Open Tue & Thu (055 854 661); www.vignamaggio.com • Admission charge*

Villa di Cafaggiolo

Tiny castle commissioned from Michelozzo (1451) by Cosimo il Vecchio de' Medici. Open only for private functions, although you can visit the gardens by appointment. ◈ *Outside Barberino di Mugello • Map E2 • Open by appointment (055 849 8103), www.castellodicafaggiolo.it*

Gardens, Villa Garzoni

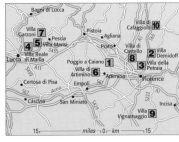

For more about Tuscany's architectural highlights See p53

Left **Montalcino label** Centre **Wine barrels** Right **Vino Nobile**

10 Wine Houses

1 Antinori (Chianti)

The Antinori Marquises have been making wine since 1385, producing more than 15 million bottles annually of some of Italy's most highly ranked and consistently lauded wines. You can sample their *vini* at Florence's Cantinetta Antinori *(see p83).*

Wine cellar, Montepulciano

2 Avignonesi (Montepulciano)

The Falvo brothers were key in reviving the quality and raising the status of Vino Nobile in the 1990s. The huge estate also produces vintages made with Merlot and Cabernet, and one of Tuscany's finest Vin Santoe. A classy show-room/free tasting bar is in Monte-pulciano. ⊗ *Map F4 • Via Gracchiano nel Corso 91 • www.avignonesi.it*

3 Castello di Brolio (Chianti)

The estate that invented mod-ern Chianti Classico is back in the Ricasoli family after years under Seagram's, and the wines have improved vastly. "Iron Baron" Bettino Ricasoli, Italy's second prime minister, perfected the formula here. *(See also p36.)*

4 Banfi (Montalcino)

Massive American-owned estate founded in 1978, producing scientifically perfect wines and a massive Brunello *riserva*. There's a huge shop and *enoteca* and a small glass and wine museum. ⊗ *Map E4 • www.castellobanfi.com • Call ahead for guided tours (0577 840 111)*

5 Monsanto (Chianti)

Full-bodied wines from the estate that was the first, in 1968, to make a single *cru* Chianti and a 100 percent Sangiovese Chianti. *(See also p36.)*

6 Poggio Antico (Montalcino)

One of the least pretentious major Montalcino vineyards, producing an award-winning velvety Brunello. ⊗ *Map E4 • 0577 848 044 • www.poggioantico.com*

7 Poliziano (Montepulciano)

Federico Carletti has made Poli-ziano one of the top producers in Montepulciano, the first to introduce the *cru* concept

Wine shop in Montalcino

Vineyard, near Fonterutoli

(grapes from a single vineyard) to Vino Nobile with Vigneto Caggiole. The vineyards are private, but there is a sales outlet with free tastings. ◈ Map F4 • Piazza Grande

8 Marchesi de' Frescobaldi (Chianti Rufina/Montalcino)

The Frescobaldi Marquises, Tuscany's largest private winemaking concern, have been viticulturalists for 30 generations (England's Henry VIII kept some stock on hand). One of the first to experiment with non-native grapes (Pinots, Cabernet Sauvignon, Chardonnay, Merlot). You can visit several estates. ◈ Map E4 • www.frescobaldi.it

9 Fonterutoli (Chianti)

Highly regarded estate in the Mazzei family since 1435, centred around a medieval village with a laid-back bar (in the osteria) for tippling. Recent vintages of the Chianti, Siepi and Brancaia have won the top Italian rankings. (See also p36.)

10 Tenuta di Capezzana (Carmignano)

A vineyard since 804, Capezzana single-handedly created the Carmignano DOC by adding 15 percent Cabernet to the otherwise Sangiovese mix. They also make a rosé version called Vin Ruspo. Book ahead for tastings. ◈ Map D3 • Direct sales 8:30am-12:30pm and 2:30-6:30pm Mon-Fri • www.capezzana.it

Tuscan Wine Styles

1 Brunello di Montalcino
One of Italy's most powerful, complex reds, best with red meat or game. 100 percent Sangiovese Grosso (the wine was perfected accidentally when a blight killed all but this grape).

2 Vino Nobile di Montepulciano
Less complex, but more versatile, than Brunello. Chianti-like blend dominated by the Prugnolo variety.

3 Chianti Classico
Italy's most famous, oft-maligned red.

4 Vernaccia di San Gimignano
Tuscany's only white DOCG, a dry to semi-sweet pale honey elixir.

5 Sassicaia di Bolgheri
Complex, long-lived Cabernet Sauvignon.

6 Tignanello
Antinori's complex, beefy wine made with 80 percent Sangiovese, 15 percent Cabernet Sauvignon and 5 percent Cabernet Franc.

7 Chianti Rufina
Since the 18th century the most structured and highest quality Chianti.

8 Carmignano
One of world's oldest official wine areas (1716), near Prato. DOCG Chianti blend with Cabernet. Long-lived, balanced.

9 Morellino di Scansano
Maremma's big DOC red, 85–100 percent Morellino (Sangiovese).

10 Vin Santo
Sweet, golden dessert wine made from raisined grapes; aged in oak barrels.

➡ For wine and food shops in Southern Tuscany See p122

Left **Courgettes** Centre Left **Pecorino cheese** Centre Right **Local seafood** Right **Florentine cake**

Tuscan Culinary Highlights

1 Bistecca Fiorentina
A classic, super-thick, juicy T-bone steak, best cut from the famous snowy white Chiana cattle, simply brushed with olive oil and cracked pepper and grilled (medium-rare) over a wood fire.

2 Crostini
Small roundels of bread, toasted, brushed with olive oil, and garnished with a number of toppings. The most popular toppings are cubed tomatoes, or *fegatini*, a chunky fresh pâté of chicken livers, capers, onions and anchovy.

3 Ribollita
The king of Tuscan soups: a rich, wintery vegetable minestrone thickened to a stew by soaking stale bread in it overnight, re-boiling it the next day (hence the name, *ri-bollita*), pouring it over new slices of bread and liberally drizzling with fresh olive oil. The ingredients vary with whatever grandma's recipe was, but always includes at least cannellini beans and *cavolo nero* (a relative of chard), plus vegetables and herbs.

4 Pappardelle al Cinghiale
Pappardelle are Tuscany's extremely wide noodles, yellow ribbons of pasta usually folded around a sauce made from *cinghiale* (wild boar) stewed so long it falls apart. Wild boar is freshest in autumn, during the hunting season, and is also often prepared as a main course, stewed in red wine *(see p65)*.

5 Fagioli all'Uccelleto
Tuscans are nicknamed *mangiafagioli*, bean-eaters, because of their love of the white cannellini beans. Cooked *al dente* (to a hard bite) like pasta, the beans are sometimes served simply dressed in fresh olive oil and cracked black pepper, but the best preparation is *all'uccelleto*, stewed with fresh tomatoes, sage, garlic cloves, olive oil and pepper.

Fagioli all'Uccelletto

6 Trippa alla Fiorentina
Florence makes tripe tolerable by dicing it up and stewing it with tomatoes, sage and

For Tuscany's top restaurants **See pp72–3**

parmigiano cheese. You will also find carts that serve tripe sandwiches.

Wild boar dish

Cacciucco

Livorno's version of *bouillabaisse* meets *pappa al pomodoro*: a thin, *pepperoncino*-spiked tomato gruel poured over stale bread slices and a stew rich in fish and seafood. The exact recipe varies with the day's market and chef's whim, but usually incorporates some tentacles.

Pici (or Pinci)

Fat, chewy, misshapen home-made spaghetti – *appicicare* means to roll between the hands – made from only flour and water, served mainly in the hill towns south of Siena, usually in a tomato sauce.

Pecorino

Italy's finest, tastiest sheep's milk cheese was perfected by the shepherds of Pienza. It comes in various states, from soft (*non-stagionato* and *marzolino*) to harder and sharper (*semi-stagionato* and the full *stagionato*). It is sometimes preserved under ash, or wrapped in grape leaves, or dusted with *pepperoncino*. The harder types are good with red wine or grated over pasta.

Panzanella

A summertime salad of stale bread soaked in water and vinegar and topped with diced tomatoes, onions, basil and olive oil.

Tuscan Sweets

Gelato

Florence makes the world's best ice cream, much denser and tastier than the packaged, air-fluffed "ice cream" made outside Italy. Make sure it's *produzione propria* (home-made).

Cantucci

Small, hard, half-moon-shaped almond biscuits – best from Prato – called *biscotti* outside Tuscany. Dip them in *Vin Santo* (a white dessert wine).

Panforte

The world's only decent fruitcake, a dense chewy nougat studded with fruits, nuts and spices.

Torta della Nonna

The traditional, creamy "Grandmother's pie", topped with *pinoli* (pine nuts).

Ricciarelli

Thick, soft, chewy Sienese honey and almond paste cakes dusted with powered sugar.

Zuppa Inglese

Florentine version of English trifle. Rum-soaked sponge cake stained red with *alkermes* liqueur and topped with pastry cream.

Brutti ma Buoni

"Ugly but good" cakes, slightly chewy in a crisp shell.

Ossi di Morti

Airy, brittle Sienese "bones of the dead" biscuits.

Zuccotto

Florentine sponge cake stuffed with a mousse of chocolate, sweets and nuts.

Pan Pepato

Medieval forerunner to Siena's *panforte*, a dense spice cake sweetened with fruits and honey.

 For the best Tuscan wines **See pp62–3**

Left **Pisa's game** Centre **Horseman's symbol, Siena** Right **Knights, Arezzo**

Festivals

Siena's Palio

Since the Middle Ages, Siena has staged a bareback horse race around the Campo *(above)*. Preparations and festivities last for a week. On the day of the race you can stand in the Campo's centre for free or buy a seat ticket (months in advance) from any business ringing the piazza. Enjoy the pageantry and *sbandieratori* (flag tossers), before glimpsing the furious, 90-second race. ◈ Map E4 • Piazza del Campo Siena • 2 Jul, 16 Aug

Prato's Display of the Virgin's Girdle

When the Virgin was assumed, body and soul, to Heaven, Doubting Thomas was sceptical, so she handed him down her girdle as proof of her ascent. A Prato Crusader brought the belt back as the dowry of a Thomas descendant, it was encased in a glass and gold reliquary, and locked in the Duomo. Five times a year the bishop shows it to crowds thronging the piazza and church, and lets a line-up of the faithful kiss the case. A procession is then led by musicians dressed in Renaissance-style costumes. ◈ Map D2 • Duomo, Prato • Easter, 1 May, 15 Aug, 8 Sep, 25 Dec

Arezzo's Giostra del Saracino

A horseback jousting contest played in medieval costume on the sloping Piazza Grande. It's the only joust in Tuscany where the target can hit back – the stylized "Saracen" is allowed to turn and knock the rider as he gallops past. ◈ Map F3 • Piazza Grande, Arezzo • 3rd Sun in Jun, 1st Sun in Sep

Florence's Calcio Storico

Football without the rules, between Florence's four traditional neighbourhoods. This violent game in Renaissance costume is usually played on the

Florence's no-nonsense football

Jousting, Arezzo

dusty Piazza Santa Croce, with matches in past years taking place in Piazza Signoria or the Boboli Gardens. ◎ *Piazza Santa Croce, Florence • Map P4 • 16–29 Jun*

Viareggio's Carnevale

Viareggio's carnival may lack the costumed balls of Venice, but their parade of elaborate floats is almost as famous. ◎ *Map C2 • Viale Carducci and Viale Marconi, Viareggio • Shrove Tuesday, and weekends in Lent*

Florence's Scoppio del Carro

White oxen pull a firework-laden cart from the baptistry's *Gates of Paradise* to the Duomo. During Easter mass, a mechanical dove sails on a wire down the nave and through the door to ignite the cart in an explosion of noise and colour. ◎ *Piazza di S. Giovanni, Florence • Map M3 • Easter Sun*

Florence's Maggio Musicale

May brings concerts, plays and recitals to Florence's theatres, churches and public spaces. Best of all are those held under the stars in the ancient Roman theatre high above the city in Fiesole. Check the

festival website for schedules. ◎ *Various venues • May-Jun • www.maggiofiorentino.com*

Montalcino's Sagra del Tordo

Montalcino celebrates hunting season by throwing a food festival in the medieval *fortezza*, roasting thousands of thrushes on spits over open fires, boiling up vats of polenta and washing it all down with Brunello wine. ◎ *Map E4 • Fortezza • Last weekend in Oct*

Montepulciano's Bravio delle Botti

After a week of medieval pageantry, festivities and feasting, costumed two-man teams from Montepulciano's eight neighbourhoods prove their racing prowess by rolling hefty barrels up this hill town's meandering, often steep main street to the piazza at the top. ◎ *Map F4 • Main drag • Last Sun in Aug*

Pisa's Gioco del Ponte

Pisan residents from either side of the Arno have always been rivals, and they fight it out by dressing in Renaissance costume and staging an inverse tug-of-war on the city's oldest bridge, competing to push a giant, leaden cart over the bridge to the other team's side. ◎ *Map C3 • Ponte di Mezzo • Last Sun in Jun*

Left **Monte Argentario** Right **Beachside restaurant, Elba**

TOP 10 Spas and Resorts

Spa, Montecatini Terme

1 Montecatini Terme
A little overbuilt, but still the best place in Italy for grandiose, Liberty-style thermal establish-ments: drink Terme Tettuccio's waters for your liver, wallow in Terme Leopoldine's mud for your skin. Also take the funicular to the medieval hill town of Montecatini Alto. *(See also p108.)* ✪ *Map D2*
• *Viale Verdi 41, Montecatini Terme • 800 132 538 • www.termemontecatini.it*

2 Viareggio
Southernmost Riviera-style resort on the coast, a mix of grand old buildings and simple tourist hotels. The promenade is lined with restaurants and shops on one side, and a crowded but sandy beach on the other (all stretches are privately run: you pay for a chair and umbrella). Not the cleanest water, but the calm sea and sandy beach are good for children. *(See also p107.)* ✪ *Map C2*

3 Saturnia: Cascate del Gorello
After Saturnia's sulphur-laden hot spring bursts out of the ground it rushes over a long slope of open-air whirlpools, a rough staircase of waterfalls and small azure pools. There, you can lie back in the warm, bubbly waters and relax. *(See also p127.)* ✪ *Map E6*

4 Forte dei Marmi
One of the string of impecca-ble, regimented-umbrella beaches along the northern Versilia, Forte dei Marmi is built around a 15th-century marble port. It stands out for its fine sands, Grand Ducal fort (1788) and the summer villas of well-to-do Italians and minor nobility hidden amid the pines. *(See also p109.)* ✪ *Map C2*

5 Monsummano Terme
A natural sauna formed from a series of subterranean caves above a sulphurous under-ground lake, filled with hot mineral-laden vapours. *(See also p109.)* ✪ *Map D2*
• *Via Grotta Giusti 1411*
• *0572 907 71*

Beach resort, Viareggio

Saturnia spa

6 Elba

Italy's third largest island offers Tuscany's best all-around coastal holiday – sandy beaches, water sports, fishing villages, resorts and vineyards. Sightseeing takes in forts, museums and mine tours devoted to the island's mineralogical wealth (discovered by the Etruscans, Elba's iron armed the Roman legions). There are also two villas left from the 11 months Napoleon lived here in exile. *(See also p125.)* ✪ *Map C5*

7 Chianciano Terme

It is fortunate that the spa waters of Acqua Santa clean the liver, for Chianciano lies at the end of a wine road from Montalcino past the Chianti and Montepulciano. This group of thermal spas – with waters and mud packs to invigorate the body – is linked to the hill town of Chianciano Alto by a long string of hotels. ✪ *Map F4* • *www.chiancianoterme.com*

The seaside, Elba

8 Saturnia Spa

The four-star Hotel Terme di Saturnia is built around this sulphur spring, whose warm waters and mineral-rich mud are held to aid the skin and respiratory system. A fitness centre is attached to the hotel, and there are also opportunities for riding. *(See also p127.)* ✪ *Map E6* • *0564 600 800* • *www.termedisaturnia.it*

9 Punta Ala

This is little more than a modern yacht marina backed by some classy hotels with private beaches. Nearby there is riding on offer and one of Tuscany's toughest, and prettiest, golf courses amid pine groves sloping down to the sea. ✪ *Map D5*

10 Monte Argentario

A mountainous peninsula covered in ilex and olives, and rimmed with isolated beaches. The trendier of its two towns is southerly Porto Ercole, where Caravaggio gasped his last. It retains a fishing village air. Porto Santo Stefano is a slightly larger, more middle-class resort town and main fishing port. *(See also p125.)* ✪ *Map E6*

🔟 Tuscany for Children

Siena's Duomo

1 Climbing the Towers and Domes

From the Duomo's dome in Florence to countless belltowers, Tuscany offers dozens of fun scrambles up to dramatic lookout points, many reached via tight, evocatively medieval stairs.

2 Exploring Tombs

Crawling through the ancient tunnels and tombs left by the Etruscans makes for a slightly spooky Indiana Jones-style adventure. The best are in the Maremma around Sorano, Sovana and Pitigliano (see pp125–7), and near Chiusi (p120).

3 Florence's Museo dei Ragazzi

Not a place but a series of daily, rotating workshops at the Palazzo Vecchio (see p78), Science Museum (p49) and Museo Stibbert (opposite). Children can explore hidden parts of the Palazzo Vecchio, play with Galilean telescopes, and dress up as Medici progeny. 🔗 www.museoragazzi.it

4 Saturnia Hot Springs

Sit back and relax in a warm sulphur pool while your offspring splash and make Italian friends in this beautiful open-air slice of Paradise. But keep little ones away from the upper parts of the stream where the current is very strong. (See pp68–69, p127).

5 Biking Lucca's Walls

Tool around the top of the city's massive 16th-century ramparts shaded by trees, and peek down into elaborate gardens.

6 Pinocchio Park, Collodi

The hometown of Pinocchio author Carlo "Collodi" Lorenzini has a small theme park. 🔗 Off the S435 outside Collodi • Map D2 • Open 8:30am–sunset daily • Admission charge

7 San Gimignano

The Town of Towers (see pp18–19) looks as Tolkeinesque as they come, a medieval fairy-tale city full of towers to climb, alleys to explore and a half-ruined fortress to clamber about. The torture museum stuffed with gruesome instruments also appeals to children.

Etruscan tomb in the Maremma

San Gimignano

Museo Stibbert, Florence

Quirky, private museum of armour. The 16th-century Florentine armour is arranged as a mounted army marching through the largest room. ◈ *Via F. Stibbert, 26 • Map E3 • 055 475 520 • www.museostibbert.it • Open 10am–1pm Mon–Wed, 10am–5pm Fri–Sun • Admission charge*

Toddlers room, Ludoteca Centrale, Florence

Ludoteca Centrale, Florence

Best suited to toddlers and small children, the courtyards of Europe's oldest foundling hospital house a selection of toys. An adult must accompany your children. ◈ *Piazza della SS. Annunziata 13 • Map P1–2 • Free*

Giardino dei Tarocchi

Odd sculpture garden of giant Tarot card images mosaicked with Gaudí-esque coloured tile chips. Niki de Saint Phalle, the artist, recently passed away, but her work goes on. ◈ *Garavicchio di Capalbio • Map E6 • 0564 895 122 • Open mid-May to mid-Oct: 2:30– 7:30pm Mon–Sat; Nov–May open 1st Sat of month (free) • Admission charge*

Tips for Families

1 Try Picnicking
It saves money, makes for a fun outing, lets the children eat what they want, and gives them a break from all those restaurants where they have to be on their best behaviour.

2 Order Half-Portions
A *mezza porzione* for smaller appetites costs less.

3 Share a Room
An extra bed costs at most 35% more; cots and baby cribs even less.

4 Make a Base
Stay in one hotel or apartment and make day-trips. Changing hotels is a time-consuming hassle, and weekly rates are cheaper.

5 Sightseeing Discounts
Ridotto tickets are for students and under 18s. Admission may be free under age 6, 12 or even 18 (especially for EU citizens).

6 Train Discounts
With the "Offerta Famiglie" for groups of two adults and one child under 12, the child travels free, although extra services, such as sleeping cars, cost the regular price.

7 Rent a Car
One car is cheaper than four sets of train tickets.

8 Gelato Breaks
Don't over-pack your itinerary. Take time to enjoy the ice cream instead.

9 Use Riposo Wisely
Sightseeing is exhausting. Therefore, do as the Italians and take a nap after lunch.

10 Relax
Italy is a multigenerational culture, accustomed to welcoming travelling clans. And a child attempting Italian is a great icebreaker with locals.

Left **La Cantinetta di Rignana** Centre **Cibrèo, Florence** Right **Dorandò, San Gimignano**

🔟 Restaurants

Cibrèo, Florence

1 Cibrèo, Florence

Florence's best restaurant has a relaxed elegance fostered by the chatty waiting staff and décor. They prepare traditional dishes, but with no pasta or roast meats, and they do not spare the *peperoncino*. The trattoria branch on Via de' Macci has a shorter menu from the same kitchen, but the prices are much lower *(see p83)*.

2 Il Latini, Florence

This is the archetypal Tuscan trattoria. You have all the elements: communal tables under *prosciutto* hamhocks hanging from beams, a cornucopia of appetizers and pastas and platters piled with roast meats, desserts, grappa and wine. The drawback is that there is always a crowd at the door *(see p83)*.

3 Gambero Rosso, San Vincenzo

Fulvio Pierangelini's internationally renowned restaurant

has an understated but picturesque dining room with spectacular views of the Tyrrhenian Sea. The Italian cuisine is superb, combining magnificent classic dishes with delightful and innovative new ones, including excellent local seafood *(see p129)*.

4 Dorandò, San Gimignano

This elegant stone-walled restaurant keeps traditional Sangimignanese recipes alive, resurrecting superbly prepared, tasty dishes from the Middle Ages and Renaissance. They even claim that some of their dishes date back to the Etruscan era. The menu explains each in detail *(see p117)*.

5 La Buca di Sant'Antonio, Lucca

The best food in Lucca since 1782. Here you will find a series of rooms hung with old kitchen implements and musical instruments. You will experience the friendliest professional welcome of any fine restaurant in Tuscany, and, of course, excellent Lucchese cooking *(see p111)*.

Dorandò, San Gimignano

6 Trattoria le Cave di Maiano, near Fiesole

High in the breeze-kissed hills above Florence, this is the

Florentines' favourite escape for long lunches on the outdoor linden pergola-shaded terrace. In cold weather, head inside the wood-beamed dining room for well-prepared regional specialities. ◉ *Via Cave di Maiano 16* • *Map E2* • *055 59 133* • *Open 12.45–3:30pm, 7:45pm–midnight* • *€€€€ (for price categories see p83)*

La Cantinetta di Rignana, near Greve in Chianti

This establishment is set amid vineyards, miles from anywhere along winding dirt roads – a complete countryside trattoria experience. Curing meats hang in the doorway and Madonna and Child icons and copper pots pepper the walls. The homemade pastas and grilled meats are delicious. There is also a glassed-in verandah for summertime dining *(see p97)*.

La Buca di San Francesco, Arezzo

Mario de Filippis's family has run this Arezzo culinary landmark in the basement of a 14th-century *palazzo* for over 70 years. The dishes are solidly traditional Tuscan – try the *saporita del buonconte*, a medieval soldier's stew of assorted meats and leftovers. The portions are wonderfully generous *(see p105)*.

Il Latini, Florence

Ristorante Fiorentino, Sansepolcro

Sansepolcro's best restaurant is nearly 200 years old – a homey, wood-ceilinged trattoria of Tuscan cuisine. The owner prefers to rhapsodize about what's best in the kitchen today rather than handing you a menu, and enjoys discussing the works of Piero della Francesca *(see p105)*.

Trattoria Sant'Omobono, Pisa

Simple Pisan home cooking at the outdoor market. The menu is full of Pisan favourites like *baccalá* (salt cod) and *brachetti alla renaiola*, an ancient recipe of pasta squares in puréed turnip greens and smoked fish. ◉ *Piazza Sant'Omobono 6* • *Map C3* • *050 540 847* • *Closed Sun* • *€€ (for price categories see p83)*

La Buca di Sant'Antonio, Lucca

Following pages **Trattoria doors**

AROUND TUSCANY

TUSCANY'S TOP 10

Left **Café terrace** Centre **Houses, Ponte Vecchio** Right **Traditional Florentine dress**

Florence

FLORENCE IS THE CRADLE *of the Renaissance, the city of Michelangelo's* David *and Botticelli's* Birth of Venus. *It was here that the Italian language was formalized and its literature born under the great poet Dante. Here enlightened Medici princes ruled: Lorenzo the Magnificent encouraged a teenage Michelangelo to pick up a hammer and chisel, and Cosimo II protected Galileo from the Inquisition. If you feel overloaded with art, explore Dante's medieval neighbourhood or the Oltrarno artisan and antiques quarter across the river; stroll around the Boboli Gardens, or venture to hilltop Fiesole (see p93).*

Left **The Uffizi, seen from across the River Arno** Right **Apse end and dome, the Duomo**

Sights in Florence

1. The Uffizi
2. The Duomo Group
3. Pitti Palace
4. Galleria dell'Accademia
5. Santa Croce
6. Ponte Vecchio
7. San Marco
8. Palazzo Vecchio
9. Piazza della Signoria
10. Il Bargello

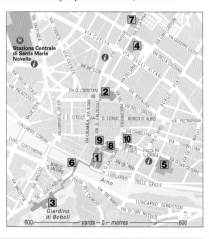

For more on Florence See pp8–17 and 44–5

1 Uffizi

The greatest gallery of Renaissance art on earth, a veritable living textbook of Western art's most shining moments, showcasing masterpieces from Giotto and Botticelli through Michelangelo, Raphael and Leonardo da Vinci to Titian, Caravaggio and Rembrandt. *(See pp8–11.)*

2 The Duomo Group

Florence's religious heart: Giotto's lithe belltower, the Baptistry's *Gates of Paradise* and Byzantine mosaics, and the Duomo museum's Michelangelo and Donatello sculptures – all lorded over by Brunelleschi's dome, a miracle of Renaissance engineering and architecture. *(See pp12–13.)*

3 Pitti Palace

This brawny Mannerist mansion served as Florence's royal home from 1560 until the 1860s, when Florence did a stint as Italy's capital. Backed by the elaborate Boboli Gardens, the palace's seven museums include the excellent Galleria Palatina of late Renaissance/early Baroque painting. *(See pp14–17.)*

4 Galleria dell'Accademia

Michelangelo's proud *David* (1501–4) stands pensively at the end of a corridor lined by the artist's *Slaves*. The plaster

Sala di Giove, Pitti Palace

casts crowding one long room hint that this is still a fine arts academy (the statues' black "pimples" are reference points to help students copy the works). *(See p48.)*

5 Santa Croce

Florence's "Westminster Abbey" contains the tombs of such Tuscan geniuses as Michelangelo and Galileo, as well as Giotto frescoes and a renowned leather school. Off the lovely cloisters are a Renaissance chapel designed by Brunelleschi (decorated by Luca della Robbia), and a small museum with a *Last Supper* by Taddeo Gaddi and Cimabue's *Crucifix*, restored after the infamous 1966 flood. *(See p44.)*

Left **Inner courtyard, Pitti Palace** Right **The tomb of Michelangelo, Santa Croce**

Left **Ponte Vecchio** Right **Courtyard, Palazzo Vecchio**

Ponte Vecchio

The shops hanging from both sides of Taddeo Gaddi's 1354 "old bridge" have housed gold- and silversmiths since Ferdinando I evicted the butchers in the 16th century (his private corridor from the Uffizi to the Pitti passed overhead, and he couldn't stand the smell). Even the Nazis, blowing up bridges to slow the Allied advance, found the span too beautiful to destroy and instead took down the buildings at either end. ✪ *Via Por S. Maria/Via Guicciardini • Map M4–5*

Piazza della Signoria

San Marco

Cosimo il Vecchio de' Medici commissioned Michelozzo to build this Dominican monastery in 1437. This was Fra Angelico's home *(see p50)*. He frescoed his brothers' cells with devotional images and left a plethora of golden altarpieces now housed downstairs near Ghirlandaio's *Last Supper* in the refectory. Fra Bartolomeo's portrait of Savonarola hangs in the "Mad Monk's" room, beside a scene of the theocrat's fiery death *(see box)*. ✪ *Piazza di S Marco 1 • Map N1 • Open 8:15am–1:50pm Mon–Fri, 8:15am–6:50pm Sat, 8:15am–7pm Sun; closed 2nd, 4th Mon and 1st, 3rd, 5th Sun of month • Admission charge*

The Bonfire of the Vanities

Puritanical preacher Girolamo Savonarola took advantage of a weak Medici to seize power in 1494. The "Mad Monk's" reign peaked in 1497 when his bands of boys looted wealthy houses to create a giant "Bonfire of the Vanities" on Piazza della Signoria. A year later, under threat of excommunication, Florence burned Savonarola himself at the stake on the same spot.

Palazzo Vecchio

Arnolfo di Cambio's mighty town hall (1299–1302) is still Florence's seat of government. Cosimo I hired Vasari to redecorate in the 1540s, frescoing a Medici marriage around Michelozzo's 1453 courtyard and swathing the gargantuan Sala dei Cinquecento with an apotheosis of the Medici dynasty. Francesco I shut himself away from matters of state in his Studiolo to conduct scientific experiments. ✪ *Piazza della Signoria 1 • Map N4 • Open 9am–7pm Fri–Wed and 9am–2pm Thu (extended hours Mon and Fri during summer) • Admission charge*

Piazza della Signoria

Florence's public living room and outdoor sculpture gallery.

Michelangelo called Ammannati's *Neptune* fountain a "waste of good marble". Lining the Palazzo Vecchio's *arringheria* – the platform from which orators "harangued" the crowds –

Sculpture by Cellini, Il Bargello

are copies of Donatello's *Marzocco* (Florence's leonine symbol) and *Judith*, and Michelangelo's *David*. The only original, Bandinelli's *Hercules* (1534), was derided by Cellini as a "sack of melons". Orcagna's lovely 14th-century Loggia dei Lanzi shelters Cellini's masterpiece *Perseus* (1545) and Giambologna's *Rape of the Sabine Women* (1583). ◈ Map N4

Il Bargello

Florence's sculpture gallery, installed in a medieval town hall and prison, contains early Michelangelos, Mannerist Giambologna's gravity-defying *Flying Mercury* (1564) and the city's best Donatello collection, including Davids in marble and bronze (the first nude since antiquity) and a puzzled *St George* (1416). ◈ *Via del Proconsolo 4 • Map N4 • Open 8:15am–1:50pm; closed 1st, 3rd, 5th Sun and 2nd, 4th Mon of month • Admission charge*

Buskers, Piazza della Signoria

The Best of Florence in One Day

Morning

Book your **Accademia** tickets (055 294 883) *(see p48)* for 8:30am and spend a leisurely 90 minutes perusing the paintings and Michelangelo statues. On your way to the **Duomo** *(see pp12–13)*, stop at Carabé, Via Ricasoli 60r, for a Sicilian *gelato*; later you can compare this milk-based treat to the Florentine milk-and-yolk version.

Be at the **Museo dell'Opera del Duomo** around 10:30, then head for the **Duomo** itself: climb the dome for stupendous views. Pop into the **Baptistry** for its Byzantine mosaics and bronze doors.

Stroll the Via dei Calzaiuoli and turn left onto Via dei Cimatori for lunch on-the-go from **I Fratellini** *(see p82)*, nibbling your sandwich and sipping wine while lounging on the cobbled street.

Afternoon

During *riposo*, when much is closed, trek over to **Santa Croce** *(see p44)* to pay your respects to the artistic luminaries buried there, and browse the leather shop. On your way back to the heart of town, stop at **Vivoli**, Florence's best *gelato* parlour at Via Isole delle Stinche 7r, for a fortifying triple scoop.

Have **Uffizi** reservations *(see pp8–11)* for 4pm: this will give you a good three hours to commune with the masters of the Renaissance. Overloaded with art, stroll across the **Ponte Vecchio** in the twilight, pause to gaze up the Arno, and plunge into the **Oltrarno** district to find a good restaurant for dinner.

Left **Museo Archeologico** Centre **Palazzo Medici-Riccardi** Right **Museo Horne**

TOP 10 The Best of the Rest

The Churches
Florence's major churches are covered fully on pp44–5, and the cathedral on pp12–13.

Museo Archeologico
Etruscan artifacts include a silver Antioch amphora, wooden Hittite chariot and the Roman bronze *Idolino*. *(See also p40.)* ◈ *Via della Colonna 36 • Map P2 • Open 2–7pm Mon, 8:30am–7pm Tue and Thu, 8:30am–2pm Wed and Fri–Sun • Admission charge*

Palazzo Medici-Riccardi
A must-see in this Medici palace of 1444 are the chapel's 360-degree frescoes by Benozzo Gozzoli. ◈ *Via Cavour 3 • Map N2 • Open 9am–7pm Thu–Tue • Admission charge*

Casa Buonarroti
Michelangelo's nephew's house. Carvings by the master are on display. ◈ *Via Ghibellina 70 • Map P4 • Open 9:30am–2pm Mon, Wed–Sat (to 4pm Sun) • Admission charge*

Spedale degli Innocenti
Brunelleschi's portico is studded with terracotta foundlings by Andrea della Robbia. The Pinacoteca inside houses paintings by Botticelli and Ghirlandaio. ◈ *Piazza SS. Annunziata 12 • Map P2 • Open 8:30am–2pm Thu–Tue • Admission charge*

Museo Horne
This Englishman's private collection includes works by Giotto and Beccafumi. ◈ *Via dei Benci 6 • Map N5 • Open 9am–1pm Mon–Sat • Admission charge*

Piazzale Michelangelo
Sweeping, postcard-ready panoramas of Florence. ◈ *Piazzale Michelangelo • Map Q6*

Cenacolo di Sant'Apollonia
Andrea del Castagno's dramatic 1450 *Last Supper*. Note the turbulent marble panel behind the heads of Jesus and Judas. ◈ *Via XXVII Aprile 1 • Map N1 • Open 8:15am–1:50pm; closed 1st, 3rd, 5th Sun and 2nd, 4th Mon of month • Admission charge*

Museo Stibbert
Wacky museum renowned for its armour collections. *(See p71.)*

Casa di Dante
Though a neighbour, Dante didn't live here, but the house is filled with documents recreating medieval Florence. His beloved Beatrice is buried in the tiny church across the street. ◈ *Via S. Margherita 1 • Map N3 • Open 10am–5pm Tue–Sat, 10am–1pm Sun (until 4pm first Sun of month) • Closed last Sun of month*

Share your travel recommendations on traveldk.com

Left **San Lorenzo market** Centre **Gucci** Right **Pineider stationery shop**

TOP 10 Shopping

1 San Lorenzo Market
A famous outdoor market offering leather goods, fashion items and marbled paper. The adjacent food market is open every morning except Sunday. ◈ *Around Piazza di San Lorenzo • Map M2 • Open 8am–8pm • Closed Mon Nov–Feb*

2 Ferragamo
Flagship store (and museum) for the firm that made cobbling an art form during Hollywood's golden age. ◈ *Via dei Tornabuoni 4r–14r • Map M3 • Open 10am–7:30pm Tue–Sat, 3:30–7:30pm Mon; Museum: 10am–6pm Wed–Mon (admission charge)*

3 Gucci
Former saddlemaker Guccio Gucci opened this leather-goods shop in 1904. ◈ *Via dei Tornabuoni 10r • Map M3 • Open 10am–7pm Tue–Sat, 3–7pm Mon, 2–7pm Sun*

4 Enoteca Alessi
This sweet shop's basement wine merchant's is the best in town. ◈ *Via delle Oche 27–29r • Map N3 • Open 9am–1pm, 4–8pm Mon–Sat*

5 Pitti Mosaici
Highest-quality *pietre dure* – "mosaics" of semi-precious stones. ◈ *Piazza dei Pitti 23r–24r • Map L5 • Open 9am–7pm daily • Closed Sun in winter*

6 Emilio Pucci
Pucci has had a fashion house in Florence for decades, offering daring prints. ◈ *Via Tornabuoni 22r • Map M3 • Open 10am–7pm Mon–Sat*

7 La Botteghina
Excellent hand-painted ceramics from some of central Italy's best artisans. ◈ *Via Guelfa 5r • Map M1 • Open 10am–1:30pm, 4–7:30pm Mon–Fri, 10am–1:30pm Sat*

8 Casa dei Tessuti
Wonderful selection of textiles, including designer names. Occasional talks on Florence are held in the shop. ◈ *Via dei Pecori 20–24r • Map M3 • Open 10am–1pm, 3–7pm Tue–Sat, 3–7pm Mon*

9 Leather School of Santa Croce
High-quality, butter-soft leather. Artisans will personalize your purchase in gold leaf. ◈ *Piazza di Santa Croce (inside church); Sun enter at Via di San Giuseppe 5r • Map P4 • Open 9:30am–6pm Mon–Sat*

10 Pineider
Stationery store of choice for celebrity and royalty. ◈ *Piazza della Signoria 13r • Map N4 • Open 10am–7:30pm Tue–Sat, 10am–2pm, 3:30–7:30pm Sun, 3:30–7:30pm Mon*

➤ *For more on shopping in Tuscany* See p122

Left **Gilli café** Centre **Cantinetta del Verrazzano** Right **Giubbe Rosse**

ᴛᴏᴘ10 Cafés and Bars

1 Gilli
Risorgimento intellectuals met under this historical café's stuccoed ceilings in the 1850s and 1860s to discuss the unification of Italy. ◈ *Piazza della Repubblica 39r • Map M3 • €€€*

2 Giubbe Rosse
The waiters' *giubbe rosse* (red jackets) recall Garibaldi's glory days; and it is here that Florence's Futurists used to meet. The café's artistic associations persist: literary competitions are still hosted here. ◈ *Piazza della Repubblica 13–14r • Map M3 • €€*

3 Rivoire
Soak up Italy in style at a classy café with tables right on the Piazza della Signoria. ◈ *Piazza della Signoria/Via Vacchereccia 4r • Map N4 • Closed Mon • €€*

4 Santo Bevitore
This wine bar in a vaulted room attracts trendy locals who enjoy the wooden platters piled with meats and cheeses and the first-rate wine list. ◈ *Via Santo Spirito 64–66r • Map L4 • 055 211 264 • €€€*

5 Cantinetta del Verrazzano
Great pastries and wonderful stuffed *focaccia* sandwiches are on offer at the Cantinetta del Verrazzano, which is owned by the Chianti wine estate (*see pp36*). ◈ *Via dei Tavolini 18-20r • Map N3/4 • €*

6 Il Volpe e l'Uva
This establishment is a low-key, jazzy wine bar situated in the Oltrarno district. ◈ *Piazza dei Rossi • Map M5 • €*

7 I Fratellini
This is a traditional *fiaschetteria* – a hole-in-the-wall wine bar also serving delicious sandwiches for on-the-go street-side eating. ◈ *Via dei Cimatori 38r • Map N4 • €*

8 Pitti Gola e Cantina
A refined little wine bar with good snacks, conveniently situated just across the square from the Pitti Palace. ◈ *Piazza Pitti 16 • Map L5 • €*

9 Red Garter
Styled after a 1920s American speakeasy, often with live music in the back. ◈ *Via dei Benci 33r • Map P4 • €*

10 Fiddler's Elbow
Not wishing to miss out on the latest fashion, Florence has its very own Irish pubs; this one is the best. ◈ *Piazza Santa Maria Novella 7r • Map L3 • €*

Left **Cibrèo** Right **Bar interior**

TOP10 Restaurants

1 La Giostra
Service with a flourish from a bona fide Medici prince and his progeny. ◈ *Borgo Pinti 12r • Map P3 • 055 241 341 • €€€€*

2 Il Latini — *Good*
This eatery has *prosciutto* hanging from the rafters and serves healthy portions of traditional Tuscan food *(see p72)*. ◈ *Via dei Palchetti 6r • Map L3 • 055 210 916 • Closed Mon • €€*

3 Cibrèo
Top restaurant, favoured by intellectuals. The annexe serves a limited menu from the same kitchen at less than half the price. ◈ *Andrea del Verrocchio 8r • Map Q4 • 055 234 1100 • Closed Sun, Mon; Aug • €€€€€ (trattoria €€)*

4 Cantinetta Antinori
Wine bar/restaurant in a 15th-century palazzo. The Antinori family has been making Chianti for generations, and the produce comes from their farms. ◈ *Piazza Antinori 3 • Map L3 • 055 292 234 • €€€*

5 Casa di Dante (del Pennello)
Going since at least the 1500s, and famous for its antipasto table laden with vegetables, fish and meat. ◈ *Via Dante Alighieri 4r • Map N3 • 055 294 848 • Closed Sun, Mon • €€*

6 Caffè Bigallo Enoteca
Cosy establishment serving typical Tuscan and Mediterranean dishes. Good value set menus. ◈ *Via del Proconsolo 73/75r • Map N3 • 055 291403 • €*

7 Il Cantinone
Crostini (grilled bread topped like a pizza) and more substantial dishes at long wooden tables. ◈ *Via Santo Spirito 6r • Map L4 • 055 218898 • Closed Mon • €€*

8 Alla Vecchia Bettola
Where Florentines go to enjoy old-fashioned dishes – some not for the weak of stomach, such as *testicciole* (rice stew in a halved sheep's skull). ◈ *Viale Vasco Pratolini 3/7 • Map J5 • 055 224 158 • Closed Sun, Mon; 2 wks Aug • €€*

9 Il Pizzaiuolo
Crowded pizza parlour also serving tasty Neapolitan pasta dishes. Expect a wait even with reservations. ◈ *Via dei Macci 113r • Map Q4 • 055 241 171 • Closed Sun • €*

10 Acqua al Due
Beloved restaurant with padded benches, soft lighting and *assaggi* (tasting) dishes. ◈ *Via della Vigna Vecchia 40r • Map N4 • 055 284 170 • Open dinner only • €€*

Following pages **Ponte Vecchio, Florence**

Left **Piazza del Campo** Right **Handmade stationery, Il Papiro**

Siena

*S*IENA OFFERS THE SUNNY DISPOSITION *of a Gothic brick-built hill town to contrast with Florence's stately Renaissance marble. As a thriving medieval merchant and textile town, Siena produced a colourful, courtly Gothic school of painting as well as a building boom, but it all came to a crashing halt when the Black Death of 1348 decimated the population. Florence would forever dominate the Tuscan scene thereafter, but luckily for visitors this means that, aside from a few Baroque church façades, second-fiddle Siena didn't have the funds to overhaul its Middle Ages look.*

Left **Café culture at Il Campo** Right **The elaborate façade of the Duomo**

Sights in Siena

1. Palazzo Pubblico
2. Piazza del Campo
3. Duomo
4. Pinacoteca Nazionale
5. San Domenico
6. Santa Maria della Scala
7. Enoteca Italiana Permanente
8. Via Banchi di Sopra
9. Casa di Santa Caterina
10. Santa Maria dei Servi

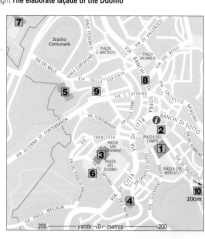

The Duomo, nave

Palazzo Pubblico

Siena's medieval town hall is a genteel brick palace. The rooms were so gorgeously decorated with early 14th-century art – including Simone Martini's *Maestà* and Ambrogio Lorenzetti's incomparable *Allegory of Good and Bad Government* – that they've been turned into a museum *(see p32)*. ⊗ *Piazza del Campo • Open daily, 10am–6:30pm • Admission charge*

Piazza del Campo

Siena's half-moon of a public square is one of the loveliest *piazze* in all of Italy, its broad slope home to the biannual Palio horse race *(see p66)* and an ever-changing cast of strollers, coffee-drinkers, readers and picnickers. So rich is it in sightseeing opportunities that it counts among Tuscany's Top 10 *(see pp30–31)*.

Duomo

This massive Gothic cathedral complex is filled with art by such masters as Michelangelo, Pisano, Pinturicchio, Bernini, Duccio and Donatello. It qualifies as one of Tuscany's Top 10 sights, and is fully covered on pages 26–7. ⊗ *Piazza del Duomo • Open daily • Admission charge*

Pinacoteca Nazionale

The Pinacoteca boasts a comprehensive collection of Sienese painting (though the masterpieces of the school are housed elsewhere). Among the earlier gems, seek out various 14th-century Madonnas by Simone Martini and Pietro Lorenzetti. Compare Beccafumi's cartoons (full-sized preparatory sketches on *cartone*, or "large paper") for the Duomo's floor panels and his Mannerist *Christ Descending into Limbo* to rival Sodoma's High Renaissance works. *(See also p49.)* ⊗ *Via S. Pietro 29 • Open daily • Admission charge*

San Domenico

This massive, architecturally uninspired brick church of 1226 contains a portrait of St Catherine by her contemporary and friend Andrea Vanni. The saint's mummified head and thumb are revered in a chapel decorated with frescoes on her life by Sodoma (1526) and Francesco Vanni. Matteo di Giovanni executed the saintly transept altarpieces. ⊗ *Piazza S. Domenico*

Left **Pinacoteca Nazionale** Right **San Domenico**

St Catherine of Siena

Italy's patron saint Caterina Benincasa (1347–80) put on a nun's veil (though she never took vows) after her first vision of Christ at the age of 8; she received the stigmata at 28. Her wisdom won her the ambassadorship to Pope Gregory XI in Avignon, where she was largely responsible for returning the papacy to Rome. In 1970 she became the first female Doctor of the Church.

Fine wines, Enoteca Italiana Permanente

comprehensive). Everything is for sale, and a selection of bottles is opened daily so that you can sample Italy's oenological bounty by the glass at small tables or outside on the terrace. 🛇 *Fortezza Medicea • Open noon–8pm Mon; noon–1am Tue–Sat*

Santa Maria della Scala

The best sections of this former hospital, which ran from the 9th century to the 1990s, are mentioned on page 28. The Renaissance frescoes in the Sala del Pellegrino depict scenes of hospital life not too different from today – a monkish surgeon doctoring an injured leg, another taking a urine sample, a third nodding off as his patient describes symptoms. Several spaces host changing exhibitions. 🛇 *Piazza del Duomo • Open 10:30am–6:30pm (to 4:30pm Nov–Mar) • Admission charge*

Enoteca Italiana Permanente

The vaulted cellars of the massive 16th-century Medici fortress are filled with Italy's national wine museum (though, since vintners send in cases only on a voluntary basis, it's far from

Via Banchi di Sopra

Siena's main *passeggiata* street (for evening promenading) is lined with palaces. Until Palazzo Pubblico was finished, the city council met in the piazza wedged between San Cristofano church and the 13th-century Palazzo Tolomei, now a bank. Further up the street, Piazza Salimbeni is flanked by Renaissance Palazzo Tantucci, Gothic Palazzo Salimbeni and Renaissance Palazzo Spannocchi. Together this group of buildings houses Monte dei Paschi di Siena, the city's chief employer and oldest bank (established 1472), and its small, worthy collection of Sienese paintings. 🛇 *Via Banchi di Sopra*

Casa di Santa Caterina

The house in which the saint was born was made a sanctuary

Left **Via Banchi di Sopra** Right **Cloisters, Casa di Santa Caterina**

For more on Siena See pp26–33

Santa Maria dei Servi

in 1466, with a modest Baroque church containing the 12th-century Pisan Crucifixion that gave Catherine the stigmata, a brick loggia (constructed in 1533 by Baldassare Peruzzi) and a small oratory with Baroque paintings by Il Riccio, Francesco Vanni and Il Pomarancio. Follow the staircase down past Catherine's cell to see if the Oratorio dell'Oca and its frescoes of angels are open.
⊗ *Costa di Sant'Agostino • Open 9am–12:30pm, 3–6pm*

10 Santa Maria dei Servi
This Romanesque church contains some fine altarpieces covering all eras of Sienese painting. Highlights are Coppo di Marcovaldo's Byzantine masterpiece *Madonna del Bordone* (1261), Matteo di Giovanni's rather creepy *Massacre of the Innocents* (1491) and Francesco Vanni's Mannerist *Annunciation*. In the transepts, the second chapels out on either side contain Gothic frescoes by Francesco and Niccolò di Segna and Pietro Lorenzetti, including another *Massacre of the Innocents*. ⊗ *Piazza A. Manzoni • Open 9am–noon, 3–6pm*

A Day in Siena

Morning

🕐 Start with the **Duomo** group *(see pp26–9)*, especially if it's winter, as the museum closes in the afternoon. Explore the Gothic nooks and Baroque crannies of the cathedral itself first, then pop across to **Santa Maria della Scala**.

Don't skip the **Museo Metropolitana** *(p28)* with works by Giovanni Pisano, Donatello and Duccio, plus fabulous views from the unfinished façade wall.

Descend the stairs to see the **Baptistry** before heading back around the other side of the Duomo for lunch at **Antica Osteria da Divo** *(p91)*.

Skip dessert so that you can pick it up at **Bini** pastry shop around the corner at Via dei Fusari 9–13 (don't eat it just yet).

Afternoon

Stroll down Via di Città, where there are plenty of attractive shops on your way to **Il Campo** *(p87)*. Either eat your pastries from Bini or grab an outdoor table at **Bar Il Palio**, Piazza del Campo 47–9. Order a coffee or glass of wine, and drink in the ambience of one of the loveliest squares in Italy.

Head inside the **Palazzo Pubblico** for the **Museo Civico** *(p32)* displaying Siena's greatest Gothic art. Exit the Campo on the north side to join the locals for a bracing espresso or Campari at famed café **Nannini** *(p90)* before continuing up Via Banchi di Sopra as part of the lively evening *passeggiata*.

Left **Ceramiche Artistiche** Centre **Antica Drogheria Manganelli** Right **Cortecci's designer clothes**

Shops, Cafés and Wine Bars

Nannini
Siena's renowned premier café roasts its own coffee and serves delicious pastries. ✎ *Via Banchi di Sopra 22–4 • €*

Ceramiche Artistiche Santa Caterina
Franca, Marcello and son Fabio produce Siena's best ceramics. The black, white and "burnt sienna" designs are based on the Duomo's floor panels. ✎ *Via di Città 51 and 74–6 • 10am–8pm daily*

Tessuti a Mano
Fioretta Bacci works her giant looms at the back, turning out colourful, unique knitwear. ✎ *Via San Pietro 7 • 10am–1pm, 1:30–7pm Mon–Fri, 1:30–5pm Sat*

Siena Ricama
Bruna Fontani's exquisite embroidery and needlepoint is inspired by medieval Sienese art, from illuminated manuscripts to Lorenzetti frescoes. ✎ *Via di Città 61 • 9:30am–1pm, 2:30–7pm Mon–Fri, 9:30am–1pm Sat*

Antica Drogheria Manganelli
Speciality Sienese foods (cookies, wines, preserves, cheeses, salamis) in a well-preserved 1879 shop. ✎ *Via di Città 71–3 • 9am–8pm Mon–Sat, 10:30am–6:30pm Sun*

Cortecci
Men's and women's designer fashion (Armani, Gucci, Prada, Versace) plus lesser-known, more affordable labels. ✎ *Via Banchi di Sopra 27 and Il Campo 30–31 • 9:30am–1pm, 3:30–8pm Tue–Sun, 3:30–8pm Mon*

Il Papiro
Chain of stationery stores specializing in marbled paper and leather-bound blank books. ✎ *Via di Città 37 • 9:30am–7:30pm daily*

Compagnia dei Vinattieri
Innovative dishes are coupled with old favourites like *pici cacio e pepe* (pasta with *pecorino* and black pepper) at this tiny *enoteca*. Wines are its strength. Don't miss the cellar in a medieval aqueduct. ✎ *Via delle Terme 79 • 0577 236 568 • €€€*

Aloe & Wolf Gallery
This gallery/shop tucked away behind Piazza il Campo sells vintage clothing and art. ✎ *Via del Porrione 23 • 10:30am–7:30pm daily*

Louis Ciocchetti
Jewellery, watches and Etruscan reproduction jewellery – all made in Italy. ✎ *Via Banchi di Sopra 91 • 10am–7pm daily*

For more on shopping in Tuscany **See p136**

Price Categories

For a three-course meal for one with a half bottle of wine (or equivalent meal), taxes and extra charges.	€ under €25
	€€ €25–€35
	€€€ €35–€55
	€€€€ €55–€70
	€€€€€ over €70

Left **Castelvecchio** Right **Tullio ai Tre Christi**

Restaurants

Osteria Le Logge
This ancient converted pharmacy offers the best traditional cuisine and friendliest service in town. ◎ *Via del Porrione 33 • 0577 48 013 • Closed Sun • €€€*

Antica Osteria da Divo
Medieval ambience, easy-going service and modern Tuscan cooking – including a new Italian trend of pairing each main course with a side dish. ◎ *Via Franciosa 29 • 0577 284 381 • Closed Tue • €€€*

Castelvecchio
The creative Tuscan food is quite refined for the price at this intimate little place. There is a daily selection of vegetarian meals. ◎ *Via di Castelvecchio 65 • 0577 49 586 • Closed Tue, Sun (occasionally open for lunch) • €€*

Osteria del Ficomezzo
This small upstairs room has tiled floors, romantic nooks and soft music. The cook combines Tuscan ingredients in sometimes unusual ways. ◎ *Via dei Termini 71 • 0577 222 384 • Closed Sun • €€*

Tullio ai Tre Christi
This bastion of the Siena restaurant scene is a traditional trattoria with a focus on fish. ◎ *Vicolo di Provenzano 1 • 0577 280 608 • Wed–Mon • €€€*

Antica Trattoria Papei
This large family-run trattoria serves solid Tuscan dishes under beamed ceilings (avoid the modern room to the right) or on the piazza outside. ◎ *Piazza del Mercato 6 • 0577 280 894 • Closed Mon • €€*

Ai Marsili
Siena's most refined (but a bit sedate) restaurant serves Sienese dishes below a 12th-century palazzo. ◎ *Via del Castoro 3 • 0577 47 154 • Closed Mon • €€*

La Taverna del Capitano
A hand-scribbled menu of hearty dishes, with laid-back service and funky modern art. ◎ *Via del Capitano 6–8 • 0577 288 094 • 12:30–3pm, 7:30–10pm Wed–Mon • €*

Cane e Gatto
The tasting menu at this small, family-run trattoria is a great introduction to Tuscan cuisine. ◎ *Via Pagliaresi 6 • 0577 287 545 • Closed for lunch and Thu • €€€€*

Osteria La Chiacchera
Remarkably cheap and no cover charge. The *cucina povera* ("poor people's cuisine") dishes and great desserts change daily. ◎ *Costa di Sant' Antonio 4 • 0577 280 631 • €*

Note: Unless otherwise stated, all restaurants accept credit cards and serve vegetarian meals

Left **Square with fountain, Prato** Centre **Certosa del Galluzzo** Right **The Duomo, Prato**

Beyond Florence

THE LUSH HILLS AND WIDE *Arno Valley spreading out from Florence are overlooked by most travellers making a beeline for Siena and Pisa. Skip the main roads and discover the spots known only to cognoscenti and locals. There's no lovelier route to Siena than the S222 Chiantigiana through the famed terracotta centre Impruneta to the castle-topped, vine-clad hills of the Chianti wine region. Just off the road to Pisa, the towns of Prato and Pistoia would be better known for their rich heritages of Romanesque architecture and Renaissance art were they not overshadowed by their mighty neighbours. Villas built by the Medici dot the countryside northwest of town.*

Left **The Baptistry, Pistoia** Right **View from Panzano in the Chianti region**

🔟 Sights Beyond Florence

1. Chianti
2. Fiesole
3. Prato
4. Pistoia
5. Villa Poggio a Caiano
6. Borgo San Lorenzo
7. Villa Demidoff
8. Certosa del Galluzzo
9. Vinci
10. Impruneta

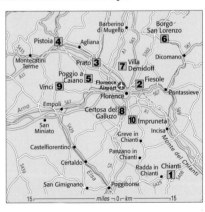

Daddi's *Story of the Holy Girdle*, Prato

Chianti
Tuscany's famous wine region has vineyards and castles, market towns and monasteries (see pp 34–7).

Fiesole
This hilltop Etruscan settlement is a short ride from Florence on a No. 7 bus. The 11th-century cathedral was assembled using ancient Roman columns, and houses Renaissance sculptures by Giovanni della Robbia and Mino da Fiesole. The remains of a Roman theatre and baths are still used for summer concerts. The steep road up to San Francesco church, with its quiet cloisters and quirky missionary museum, passes a peaceful park, shaded by ilex and peppered with water-colourists reproducing its famous view of Florence. ⊗ *Map E2 • Tourist Office: Via Portigiani 3 • 055 598 720*

Prato
The mercantile tradition of this fast-growing city dates to 15th-century financial genius Francesco Daitini, famed "Merchant of Prato" and inventor of the promissory note. His frescoed Palazzo is one of the best preserved of

its kind in Italy. Prato's best art decorates the Duomo (see p47), but the Galleria Communale has a lovely collection of early Renaissance polyptych altarpieces by such masters as Filippo Lippi and Bernardo Daddi. The half-ruined Castello dell'Imperatore (1420s), its ramparts and grassy interior now a city park, was built by Emperor Frederick II to defend the road from his German kingdom home to his lands in southern Italy. ⊗ *Map D2 • Tourist Office: Piazza delle Carceri 15 • 0574 24 112 • www.prato. turismo.toscana.it*

Pistoia
An ancient Roman town of metal workers – the industry's thin daggers, which evolved into handguns, were called *pistole* after the city. It is an artistic crossroads where the striking Romanesque stripes in San Giovanni Fuoricivitas and the Duomo (see p47) meet the Florentine Renaissance glazed terracottas festooning the Ospedale del Ceppo. Gothic art comes in the form of colourful 1372 frescoes covering the Cappella del Tau, and a Giovanni Pisano carved pulpit (1298–1301) in the church of Sant'Andrea. ⊗ *Map D2 • Tourist Office: Piazza Duomo 4 • 0573 21 622 • www.pistoia.turismo.toscana.it*

View over Fiesole

For more on northeastern Tuscany **See pp100–105**

Left **Certosa del Galluzo** Right **Collegiata, Impruneta**

Villa Poggio a Caiano

The ultimate Renaissance Medici villa. It was designed by Giuliano da Sangallo and frescoed by the likes of Filippino Lippi and Pontormo. *(See also p60.)* ✆ Map D2 • Piazza de' Medicea 14 • Open Nov–Feb: 8:30am–3:30pm; Mar, Oct: 8:15am–4:30pm; Apr, May, Sep: 8:15am–5:30pm; Jun–Aug: 8:30am–6:30pm (ticket office closes 1 hour before) • Admission charge

Borgo San Lorenzo

Medieval capital of the Mugello region, surrounded by Medici villas such as Cafaggiolo *(see p61)* and the Michelozzo-designed Castello del Trebbio (1461). In the town itself, painstakingly rebuilt after a 1919

Tabernacle of St Francis, Borgo San Lorenzo

Florentine Expansion

In 1125 Florence virtually obliterated its hilltop neighbour Fiesole and began to prowl for land. It allied with the amenable (Prato, 1351), conquered the recalcitrant (Pistoia, 1301; Pisa, 1406) and built the rest (Livorno, 1571). Three years of bloody battle finally defeated Siena (1554–7), and in 1569 the Pope named Cosimo I de' Medici Grand Duke of Tuscany.

earthquake, the 12th-century Pieve di San Lorenzo contains Renaissance altarpieces by Taddeo Gaddi and Bachiacca, apse murals by local Art Nouveau ceramics entrepreneur Galileo Chini (1906) and a damaged *Madonna* fresco by Giotto. ✆ Map E2 • Tourist Office: "Borgo Informa" Piazza Garibaldi/"Pro Loco" Via O. Bandini 6 • 055 845 6230

Villa Demidoff

The mansion is gone, but Buontalenti's fountain-filled and statue-studded Pratolino park remains a favourite excursion from Florence. *(See also p60.)* ✆ Map E2 • Pratolino • Apr–Sep: 10am–8:30pm Thu–Sun; Mar: 10am–6pm Sun; Oct: 10am–7pm Sun • Admission charge

Certosa del Galluzzo

This charterhouse, home to Carthusian monks from the 1300s to 1956, now serves the Cistercian Order. The building retains an original small monk's church, a visitable cell and peaceful Renaissance cloisters

Leonardo's model bicycle, Vinci

set with della Robbia terracotta *tondi* and a small gallery of the Pontormo frescoes (1523–5). ✪ Map E3 • Galluzzo • Open 9am–noon, 3–5pm Tue–Sun (until 6pm in summer)

9 Vinci

In 1452, on the outskirts of this unassuming medieval hill town, a bastard child was born named Leonardo, who grew up to become one of the greatest scientific minds and artistic talents in history. The 11th-century Castello Guidi now houses a Museo Vinciano devoted to over 100 models of the master's inventions. Up the road, set in an olive-clad farmscape that might have come from one of his works, is Leonardo's simple *casa natale* (birthplace). ✪ Map D2 • Tourist office: Via della Torre 11 • 0571 568 012

10 Impruneta

Terracotta-producing town with a miracle-heavy Renaissance Collegiata church. Flanking the high altar are chapels designed by Michelozzo and decorated with Luca della Robbia terracottas. The right one contains a fragment of the True Cross, the left an icon of the Virgin (supposedly painted by St Luke), which was buried here during the early Christian persecutions and ploughed up by an ox while the church foundations were being dug. Also on view are fine Baroque paintings and a Mannerist Giambologna crucifix. ✪ Map E3 • Tourist info: Piazza Garibaldi/"Pro Impruneta" • 055 231 3729

A Tour of the Region

Morning

🕐 Start with **Pistoia** (see p93) and the stupendous Gothic frescoes inside Capella del Tau (incredibly, a private owner in the 16th century whitewashed over them). Go down to zebra-striped San Giovanni Fuoricivitas for a Romanesque feast.

🍴 Pop next door into what was once part of the church but now houses the Café Valiani for flaky croissants and cappuccino. Don't dawdle: you need time for the **Duomo** (closes at noon, see p47) then Sant'Andrea (closes 12:30). Head back to the centre by way of Ospedale del Ceppo and its terracotta reliefs. Join the locals for a hearty lunch at workaday **Lo Storno** trattoria (see p97) just off the picturesque market square where medieval-style second storeys project over the ground floors of the buildings.

Afternoon

From Pistoia, it's a quick drive to **Prato** (see p93). Stop first at Palazzo Daitini's frescoes (the St Christopher by the door was a common feature, believed to help protect those leaving the house) to pay your respects to the medieval Merchant of Prato, who inscribed his account ledgers "For God and Profit".

Do the **Duomo** (see p47) and, if you have time, the adjacent Museo dell'Opera del Duomo and the Palazzo Pretorio. Grab a bag of cantucci at Antonio Mattei and clamber onto the broken ramparts of Castello dell'Imperatore for a nice view of Santa Maria delle Carceri (1485–1506), a fine High Renaissance church.

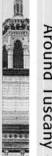

Left **Ceramiche Rampini** Centre **Macelleria Falorni** Right **Albergaccio**

Shops and Cafés

1 Ceramiche Rampini, near Radda
One of the best Italian ceramicists, producing classy and whimsical designs. You can buy anything from a single piece to a full dinner service. ◊ Map E3 • Casa Beretone di Vistarenni (road to Siena)

2 Macelleria Falorni, Greve
The ceilings at this butcher's have been hung with prosciutto and the walls festooned with salami since 1729. Good wines, too. ◊ Map E3 • Piazza Matteotti 69–71

3 The Mall, Leccio Regello, near Florence
Come here for savings on clothes, shoes and accessories by names such as Armani, Gucci, St Laurent and Bottega Veneta. The outlet centre runs a shuttle bus from Florence (055 865 7775 Mon–Fri, for bookings). The modern building is marked "café" and is 3 miles (5 km) off the main road. ◊ Map E3 • Via Europa 8 (take Incisa exit from A1)

4 Antonio Mattei, Prato
Since 1858 this shop has been making the best cantucci (biscuits) in Italy. Buy some to take back home, along with a bottle of vin santo. ◊ Map D2 • Via Ricasoli 20–22

5 Luciano Porciatti, Radda
Excellent deli with fine cheeses and meats. The nearby grocer sells wine and packaged regional foods. ◊ Map E3 • Piazza IV Novembre 1–3

6 Barberino Designer Outlet, Barberino di Mugello
Over 100 designer outlets as well as many cafés and eateries. ◊ Map E2 • Via Meucci • Closed Mon Feb–May, Oct, Nov.

7 Luca Mannori, Prato
Delicious cakes and a huge variety of chocolates are sold at this pastry shop and chocolate-makers. ◊ Map E2 • Via Lazzerini 2

8 Nuovo Mondo, Prato
Stop for delicious sweets, panini and pastries with classy service if you find yourself in this busy shopping street. ◊ Map E2 • Via Garibaldi 23 • €

9 Carlo Fagiani, Panzano
A modern showroom selling traditional leather goods. Jackets, bags and shoes made to measure. ◊ Map E3 • Via G. da Verrazano 17

10 Caffè New York, Pistoia
A great café offering a wide range of coffees, which are also for sale in interesting and unusual packaging. ◊ Map D2 • Viale Adua 5/7

Luciano Porciatti, Radda

Price Categories

For a three-course	€ under €25
meal for one with a	€€ €25–€35
half bottle of wine (or	€€€ €35–€55
equivalent meal), taxes	€€€€ €55–€70
and extra charges.	€€€€€ over €70

Left **Oltre il Giardino, Panzano** Right **Il Pirana, Prato**

Where to Eat

1 La Cantinetta di Rignana, near Greve

This is the ultimate in rural feasting: both the setting and the food are second to none *(see p73)*. ○ *Loc Rignana • Map E3 • 055 852 601 • Closed Tue • €€€*

2 Da Delfina, Artimino

One of Tuscany's finest countryside restaurants, mixing classy service with merrymaking and refined but traditional cooking. *Coniglio con olive e pinoli*, rabbit with olives and pine nuts, is a scrumptious speciality. ○ *Via della Chiesa 1 • Map D2 • 055 871 8074 • Closed Mon, Sun evening • €€€ • No credit cards*

3 La Cantinetta di Spedaluzzo, near Greve

Roadside trattoria with commanding hilltop view from the summer terrace. Serves perhaps the best *ribollita, crostini* and *tiramisu* in Tuscany. ○ *Via Mugnana 93 (S222) • 055 857 2000 • Map E3 • Closed Tue • €€*

4 Albergaccio, Castellina

A creative, nouvelle touch to refined Tuscan dishes, such as *ricotta gnocchi* under shaved black truffles and thyme. ○ *Via Fiorentina 63 • Map E3 • 0577 741 042 • €€€*

5 La Fontana, Prato

Specializes in simple, authentic Tuscan food with a variety of fragrant home-baked desserts. ○ *Via di Canneto 1 • Map D2 • 0574 27282 • €€€*

6 Oltre il Giardino, Panzano

Enjoy generous portions, intimacy and postcard views. The menu changes daily. Booking is advised. ○ *Piazza G. Bucciarelli 42 • Map E3 • 055 852 828 • Closed Mon • €€*

7 Trattoria dell'Abbondanza, Pistoia

Cosy eatery behind Piazza del Duomo serving superb Tuscan fare. ○ *Via dell'Abbondanza 10 • Map D2 • 0573 368 073 • Closed Wed, L Thu • €*

8 Baghino, Prato

Solid Tuscan and Italian dishes at the best restaurant in the historic town centre. ○ *Via dell'Accademia 9 • Map D2 • 0574 27 920 • €€€*

9 Il Pirana, Prato

One of Tuscany's best seafood restaurants. ○ *Via Valentini 110 • Map D2 • 0574 25 746 • Closed L Sat, Sun • €€€*

10 Lo Storno, Pistoia

This simple, cheerful trattoria has a weekly changing menu and documents dating it back to 1395. ○ *Via del Lastrone 8 • Map D2 • 0573 26 193 • €€*

La Cantinetta di Rignana

 Following pages **Isolated farm south of Florence**

Left **Arezzo gate** Centre **Lion relief, Cortona** Right **Locally made plate, Cortona**

Northeastern Tuscany

AREZZO'S PROVINCE STRETCHES *from the thickly forested mountains of the Casentino in the north, down the northern arm of the Arno river valley, past the hamlet of Caprese where Michelangelo was born, to the wide Chiana Valley, the regional breadbasket. Aside from the happenstance of Michelangelo's birthplace, artistically the province is dominated by two early Renaissance titans: Sansepolcro's own Piero della Francesca (see p50) in the province's northern half, and, in the south, Cortona-born Luca Signorelli (1441–1523), whose fresco technique Michelangelo later studied avidly.*

Sights in Northeastern Tuscany

1. Arezzo
2. Cortona
3. Sansepolcro
4. Monte San Savino
5. Monterchi's Madonna del Parto
6. Lucignano
7. La Verna
8. Castiglion Fiorentino
9. Poppi
10. Camáldoli

Arezzo piazza

Ristorante La Locanda nel Loggiato, Cortona

Medieval houses, Cortona

Arezzo

An Etruscan city, then ancient Roman pottery centre, Arezzo was later home to Guido Monaco, who invented modern musical notation in the 11th century, the poet Petrarch (1304–74) and Giorgio Vasari (1512–74), architect and author of the first art history text, *Lives of the Artists*.

The town's centre is the broad, sloping Piazza Grande. The bell-tower, façade and medieval Calendar reliefs of the 12th-century Santa Maria della Pieve are Lombard-Romanesque style, but the altarpiece (1320) is pure Sienese Gothic courtesy of Pietro Lorenzetti. The Duomo has excellent stained-glass windows by French master Guillaume de Marcillat, and a fresco by Piero della Francesca. The 14th-century San Francesco is graced with Piero's recently restored *Legend of the True Cross* (1448–66). ◎ *Map F3*
• *Tourist Office: Piazza della Repubblica 28*
• *0575 377 678* • *www.apt.arezzo.it*

Cortona

Cortona is the quintessential Tuscan hill town with its Etruscan tombs, medieval alleys, Renaissance art and excellent restaurants *(see pp38–41)*.

Sansepolcro

Medieval town with a reputation built around Buitoni pasta and home-grown genius Piero della Francesca *(see p50)*. The Museo Civico houses (alongside works by Signorelli and natives Santi di Tito and Raffaellino del Colle) Piero's *Madonna della Misericordia* (1445–62), *San Giuliano* fresco fragment (1455–8), and the compelling *Resurrection*. ◎ *Map F3 • Tourist office: Via Matteotti 8*
• *0575 740 536*

Monte San Savino

This ceramics town has a small pottery museum and Santa Chiara church, which contains early works in terracotta by native sculptor Andrea Sansovino (1460–1529). He also carved marble (a sarcophagus in the Pieve), designed the loggias and cloisters of Sant'Agostino and collaborated with Antonio da Sangallo the Elder on the Loggia dei Mercanti, opposite Sangallo's lovely Palazzo di Monte. ◎ *Map F4 • Tourist Office: Piazza Gamurrini 3 • 0575 849 418*

Monte San Savino

Left **Monastery at La Verna** Right **Castello di Poppi**

5 Monterchi's Madonna del Parto

Piero della Francesca's masterwork takes the unusual subject of a heavily pregnant Virgin Mary, her tired face and drooping eyes revealed by angels pulling back the curtains. It was painted in a nearby chapel, where it became a pilgrimage focus for pregnant women until it was removed to this small museum. ◈ *Map F3 • Via della Reglia 1 • 0575 70 713 • Open 9am–1pm, 2–7pm (to 6pm Oct–Mar) Tue–Sun • Admission charge*

6 Lucignano

Tiny, elliptical town, whose single street spirals to the 16th-century Collegiata church. Behind the church, the Palazzo Comunale houses a museum with late Gothic Sienese paintings and a 2m (6ft)

St Francis

Son of a wealthy Assisi merchant, Francis (1182–1226) gave up his carousing, soldiering way of life after a Crucifixion image spoke to him with an instruction to "rebuild my church". He renounced worldly goods, wrote delightful poems and preached poverty and charity – the foundation of the Franciscan Orders. In 1224, while praying on La Verna, he received history's very first stigmata.

high gold reliquary dubbed *Tree of Lucignano* (1350–1471). ◈ *Map F4*

7 La Verna

St Francis himself founded this clifftop monastery, and a Baroque frescoed corridor passes the now-enclosed cave where he slept. At the end of the corridor is the Cappella delle Stimmate, which was built over the site where the saint received his stigmata in 1224. For a sense of the saint's La Verna unencumbered by buildings, follow the path to Sasso Spico, another rocky outcrop where the holy man prayed. ◈ *Map F3 • Santuario della Verna • 0575 5341 • 7am–7pm • Free*

Lucignano rooftops

View near Monterchi

8 Castiglion Fiorentino

Off Piazza del Municipio, Sant'Agostino has a trove of paintings, starring the 13th-century *St Francis* by Margheritone d'Arezzo, Gaddi's *Madonna and Child* and Bartolomeo della Gatta's *St Francis Receiving the Stigmata*. ◎ *Map F4 • Tourist info: Piazza Risorgimento 19 • 0575 658 278*

9 Poppi

The sweetest Casentino hill town, dominated by the Castello dei Conti Guidi (1274–1300), built by Lapo and Arnolfo di Cambio, the latter architect of Florence's Palazzo Vecchio. Inside is a chapel, frescoed by Taddeo Gaddi. ◎ *Map F3*

10 Camáldoli

San Romulado established this Benedictine community in 1012, though the monastery is 15th century and the Vasari-decorated church 16th. One mile (1.6km) up a forest path lies the secluded hermitage (only men admitted), a tiny village of monkish cottages alongside a Baroque church. ◎ *Near Camáldoli • Map F2 • 0575 556 012 • www.camaldoli.it • Open winter 9am–1pm, 2:30pm–7pm; summer 9am–1pm, 2:30pm–7:30pm • Free*

A Day in Arezzo

Morning

🕐 Start at the Museo Archeologico Mecenate, a museum of corallino pottery and other ancient artifacts that stands on the former amphitheatre.

☕ Head up to Piazza Grande for a cappuccino at one of the cafés under Vasari's Loggia. Admire the square's Gothic and Renaissance palazzi before visiting Santa Maria della Pieve.

Climb up past the Casa di Petrarca (the poet's supposed house) to the Duomo and its masterful stained glass. On Thursday and Friday mornings you could first nip to the tiny Museo del Duomo to see paintings by Bartolomeo della Gatta, and Spinello and Parri Aretino.

🍴 Wander back downhill for lunch at **La Buca di San Francesco** *(see p105)*.

Afternoon

Having pre-booked (063 2810; 9am–6pm Mon–Fri, 9am–1pm Sat), head for the Piero works in **San Francesco** *(see p47)*.

🍨 Grab a heavenly *gelato* (ice cream) from **Caffè dei Costanti** *(see p104)*, and walk down Via Cavour to the Badia. Above the high altar note the trompe-l'oeil "dome" (1702) painted by Baroque master of illusion Andrea Pozzo.

Via Garibaldi leads past SS. Annunziata to the Museo Statale d'Arte Medievale e Moderna, a mix of Romanesque sculpture, majolica ceramics, and paintings by Parri Aretino, Bartolomeo della Gatta and Vasari.

Left **Antica Drogheria, Cortona** Centre **Caffè la Torre, Arezzo** Right **Buca di San Francesco, Arezzo**

Shops and Cafés

1 Prada Outlet, Montevarchi
Arrive early in the day for some incredible deals on high fashion in this back-of-a-factory complex just off the A1. ⊗ Levanella (S69) • Map E3 • 055 978 9635

2 Caffè la Torre, Arezzo
Lively café in a 14th-century palazzo right in the historic centre. It has a wonderful garden and terrace. ⊗ Corso Italia 102 • Map F3 • 0575 24728 • Open 10am–9pm Mon–Tue, Thu–Fri, Sun, 10am–1pm Sat (summer, until midnight every evening) • Closed Wed • €

3 Arezzo's Antiques Market
Italy's top monthly antiques market. Over 600 dealers crowding the Piazza Grande and streets around it. ⊗ Piazza Grande • Map F3 • Open 7:30am–3pm 1st weekend of month

4 Il Cocciaio, Cortona
Ceramics in a traditional palette of yellow, green and cream, and patterns often featuring daisies (a design first used by Gino Severini). ⊗ Via Nazionale 69/ Via Benedetti 24 • Map F4

Caffè la Torre, Arezzo

5 Antica Drogheria, Cortona
Cute boutique stuffed with wines, grappa and the health products of the Camáldolesi monks. ⊗ Via Nazionale 3 • Map F2 • Open 9am–1pm, 3–8pm

6 Sotto San Francesco, Arezzo
A plethora of wines, olive oils and local artisan products, including Aghiari lace, Monte San Savino ceramics and wrought iron. ⊗ Via di S. Francesco 5 • Map F3

7 Caffe degli Artisti, Cortona
Part locals' bar, part tourist shop hawking honey, preserves, biscuits, meats, spices and olive oils. ⊗ Via Nazionale 18 • Map F4 • Open Tue–Sun

8 Uno A Erre, Arezzo
You can buy gold jewellery direct from this world-renowned manufacturer. ⊗ Via Fiorentina 550, Strada Statale di Val d'Arno • Map F3 • Open Mon–Sat

9 Macelleria Aligi Barelli, Arezzo
Famous local butcher specializing in meats (mainly salami) from the Casentino region. Perfect for picnics. ⊗ Via della Chimera 22b • Map F3

10 Il Gelato, Arezzo
A classic gelateria. Try one of their unique homemade flavours such as pinolata (pine nuts). ⊗ Via de' Cenci 24 • Map F3 • Closed Wed

Price Categories

For a three-course meal for one with a half bottle of wine (or equivalent meal), taxes and extra charges.	€ under €25
	€€ €25–€35
	€€€ €35–€55
	€€€€ €55–€70
	€€€€€ over €70

Left **Le Tastevin, Arezzo** Right **Restaurant sign, Cortona**

Where to Eat

1 Locanda dell'Amorosa, Amorosa

Fourteenth-century farm complex and inn, with a refined restaurant in the converted stalls. The high-class Tuscan cuisine is served in a rustic, fire-warmed setting. Booking advised. ✪ *Near Sinalunga • Map F4 • 0577 677 211 • www. amorosa.it • Closed Mon • €€€€€*

2 Il Falconiere, Cortona

Silvia and Riccardo Baracchi converted the *limonaia* of their 17th-century estate into this Michelin-starred restaurant, one of the finest in the region, adding rich flourishes to the already excellent Tuscan cuisine. ✪ *San Martino in Bocena 370 (just north of Cortona) • Map F4 • 0575 612 679 • €€€€*

3 La Buca di San Francesco, Arezzo

Very friendly cellar restaurant; generous portions *(see p73)*. ✪ *Via di S Francesco 1 • Map F3 • 0575 23 271 • Closed Mon pm, Tue • €€*

4 Ristorante Fiorentino, Sansepolcro

Old-fashioned inn serving hearty food *(see p73)*. ✪ *Via L Pacioli 60 • Map F3 • 0575 742 033 • Closed Wed • €€€*

5 Preludio, Cortona

This gastronomic address in Cortona serves nouvelle Tuscan dishes in a Renaissance palazzo setting (the frescoes are modern). ✪ *Via Guelfa 11 • Map F4 • 0575 630 104 • €€*

6 La Locanda nel Loggiato, Cortona

New owners have kept prices moderate for their Tuscan cooking, despite using some expensive ingredients. The draw is the balcony setting, overlooking the main piazza. ✪ *Piazza di Pescheria 3 • Map F4 • 0575 630 575 • Closed Wed • €*

7 Le Tastevin, Arezzo

Best cooking in Arezzo, with a primarily Tuscan menu. The owner sometimes plays a little jazz at the piano, but service can be brusque. ✪ *Via de Cenci 9 • Map F3 • 0575 28 304 • Closed Tue • €€€*

8 La Grotta, Cortona

Outdoor seating on a tiny piazza, stony medieval rooms evoking that "grotto" and solid Tuscan dishes make this popular with locals and college students. ✪ *Piazza Baldelli 3 • Map F4 • 0575 630 271 • Closed Tue • €€*

9 Antica Osteria l'Agania, Arezzo

Cosy trattoria where the comfort food includes *grifi e polenta* (fatty veal stomach in polenta). ✪ *Via Mazzini 10 • Map F3 • 0575 295 381 • Closed Mon • €*

10 Totò, Lucignano

Tuscan osteria annexed to a lovely hotel. The locals give owners Boris and Beatrice *carte blanche* when they order, speci-fying only the size of meal. ✪ *Piazza Tribunale 6 • Map F4 • 0575 836 763 • Closed Tue • €€*

 Note: *Unless otherwise stated, all restaurants accept credit cards and serve vegetarian meals*

Left **Market in Lucca** Centre **Café in Lucca** Right **Leaning Tower, Pisa**

Northwestern Tuscany

T HE COASTAL NORTHWEST CORNER of Tuscany is a land of craggy mountains, wide plains and beautiful Romanesque architecture. Proud, independent Lucca, with its bicycling grandmothers and exquisite Renaissance sculpture, managed to stay a Medici-free republic until Napoleon came along. Lively university city Pisa retains the cultural heritage from the 11th–13th centuries, when its navy ruled the Western Mediterranean. Brash upstart Livorno has grown in leaps and bounds since the 16th century to become a major port. The three cities still nurse bitter rivalries.

Left **Baptistry, Pisa** Right **Monument, Livorno**

Sights in Northwestern Tuscany

1. Pisa
2. Lucca
3. Livorno
4. Viareggio
5. Garfagnana
6. Carrara
7. Montecatini Terme
8. Pontrémoli
9. Fantiscritti Marble Quarries
10. Forte dei Marmi

Pisa

Tuscany's favourite daytrip offers more than just a leaning tower. The gorgeous collection of Romanesque buildings called the "Field of Miracles" ranks among Tuscany's Top 10 sights (see pp22–5).

Lucca

Elegant small city of avid cyclists, church concerts, Romanesque façades and exquisite Renaissance sculpture. Another one of Tuscany's Top 10 (see pp42–3).

Livorno

Though Florence had already subjugated Pisa in the 16th century, Pisa's silty harbour and unsure loyalties prompted Grand Duke Cosimo I to hire Buontalenti to build him a brand-new port from scratch. Livorno and Pisa have hated each other ever since.

Livorno is Tuscany's second city, but short on sights when compared with, say, Pisa. There is just the somewhat wishfully named Venezia Nuova ("new Venice") canal district, Pietro Tacca's Mannerist masterpiece *Monumento ai Quattro Mori* (1623–6) at the port, and the Museo Civico Giovanni Fattori. The latter is devoted to native son Fattori, chief painter of the 19th-century Macchiaioli (Tuscan "impressionists"). Artist Amedeo

Roof tops, Lucca

Modigliani was also born here (but worked in Paris), as was composer Pietro Mascagni. ✎ *Map C3 • Tourist info: main booth on Piazza Cavour 6 • 0586 204 611 • www.costadeglietruschi.it*

Viareggio

Of the Versilia beach resorts, Viareggio has the most style and substance. The Liberty Style (Art Nouveau) of its many villas, cafés and buildings harkens back to the resort's heyday in the 1920s. Its carnival parade (see p67), along the popular palm-shaded seafront promenade Viale G. Carducci, is renowned throughout Italy. ✎ *Map C2 • Tourist info: Viale Carducci 10 • 0584 962 233 • www.versilia.net*

Left **Lucca** Right **Livorno port**

Left **Garfagnana Mountains** Right **Poster for Forte dei Marmi resort**

Garfagnana Region

The Serchio River Valley north of Lucca's plain is bounded on the east by the Apuan Alps, which are home to the Grotta del Vento (Cave of the Winds). To the west are the wilds of the Garfagnana Mountains. Stopping points in the region include Borgo a Mozzano, which consists of an inn and the lithe Ponte del Diavolo bridge. In legend, this was built by the Devil in exchange for the first soul to cross it (villagers sent a dog).

Today virtually forgotten, in the 19th century Bagni di Lucca was one of Europe's most fashionable spas (all the English Romantic poets came). The world's first casino opened here in 1837.

Barga's white Duomo has a marvellously detailed 13th-century pulpit carved by Guido da Como. The Este dukes once owned the 14th-century fortress of Castelnuovo di Garfagnana, and installed the poet Ludovico Ariosto as commander and toll-taker. § *Map C2–D2 • Tourist info: Lucca (see p42)*

Carrara

Carrara is a quarry town, its snowy white marble the source of grandiose sculpture from ancient Rome to Michelangelo to Henry Moore. The town's

Castelnuovo di Garfagnana

Giacomo Puccini

The operatic composer (1858-1924) was born in Lucca at Corte San Lorenzo 9. A small museum here includes the piano Puccini used to compose *Turandot*. He wrote his masterpieces *La Bohème*, *Tosca* and *Madame Butterfly* (and also hunted ducks) at his villa on the shores of Lake Massaciuccoli. The villa is also now a museum.

Duomo is pure Carrara marble, and marble-cutting shops and sculptors' studios fill the streets. On the main square, look for the plaque and relief of stone-carving tools that mark the house where Michelangelo once stayed. The Museo del Marmo features the ancient Roman altar Edicola di Fantiscritti. § *Map C2 • Tourist info: Piazza Cesare Battisti 1 • 0585 641 422 or 641 471*

Montecatini Terme

This posh, if overbuilt, thermal spa town is worth staying in to experience one of the 19th-century, Grande Dame hotels. Above the town, medieval Montecatini Alto is a favourite escape for summer breezes and cappuccino on the piazza, while nearby

Montecatini Alto

Monsummano Terme *(see p68)* has the attraction of natural cave saunas. ⓢ *Map D2 • Tourist info: Viale Verdi 66 • 0572 772 244*

Pontrémoli

Stranded up a northern spit of Tuscany is Pontrémoli and its Museo delle Statue-Stele. Some of the museum's 20-odd prehistoric *menhirs* (tombstone-like slabs) date from 3000 BC, the more elaborate ones from 200 BC. ⓢ *Map B1 • Museum: Castello di Piagnaro • 0187 831 439 • Open Tue–Sun • admission charge*

Fantiscritti Marble Quarries

Marble quarries make the Apuan Alps above Carrara appear snow-capped year round. Fantiscritti has a museum of traditional stonecutting tools, which can be reached by following the Carrione River to Vara Bridge, a former rail link to the docks that was converted to road use in 1965. ⓢ *Map C2 • 9am–dusk • Free*

Forte dei Marmi

Tiny resort favoured by jet-setters. The village is set back amid the pine forest, the beach lined with colourful little beach cabanas. ⓢ *Map C2 • Tourist info: via Franceschi 8 • 0584 80091*

Pisa and Lucca in a Day

Morning

Start your day on the "Field of Miracles" in **Pisa** *(see pp22–5)*. Admire the Pisano pulpits in the **Duomo** *(see p23)* and the perfect acoustics of the Baptistry. You can compare the artist's original sketches with repro-ductions of the finished frescoes at Museo delle Sinopie. Enjoy the cathe-dral's treasures at Museo dell'Opera del Duomo, where charts show how the Campo buildings form various perfect geometries.

Grab a bus or taxi to Pisa's great oft-missed sight, the excellent painting collection of Museo San Matteo. Stroll back along the Arno to the Ponte di Mezzo, turn right up Borgo Stretto then left into the colourful Vetto-vaglie Market, where you will find **Trattoria Sant' Omobono** *(see p73)*.

Afternoon

Catch a train or drive to **Lucca** *(see pp42–3)*, where your first stop is the **Duomo** *(see p46)*. Then climb Torre Guinigi for the panoramas.

Walk through Piazza Anfi-teatro and under the glitter-ing façade of San Frediano to see its *Miracles of San Frediano* frescoes and the shunken body of St Zita, patron saint of maids and ladies-in-waiting. Head down fashionable Via Fil-lungo for a spot of shopping and the impressive San Michele in Foro.

Finally, climb onto the city walls. If you are staying the night in Lucca, rent a bicycle to return tomorrow (the shops close at 7:30pm); if not, stroll the walls on foot.

For more on the marvels of Pisa and Lucca See pp22–5 & 42–3

Left **Shop fronts, Lucca** Centre **Bakery in Lucca** Right **Da Bruno, Pisa**

🔟 Shops and Cafés

1 Arturo Pasquinucci, Pisa
Treat yourself – or a (very good) friend – to a present from this 1870 shop, selling classy Italian kitchenware ranging from contemporary porcelain to Alessi gadgets. ⊗ Map C3 • Via Oberdan 22

2 Caffè dell'Ussero, Pisa
Look out over the Arno River and imbibe with the ghosts of Pisa's intellectual élite at one of Italy's oldest literary cafés – it opened in 1794. ⊗ Map C3 • Lungarno Pacinotti 27 • € • No credit cards

3 Carli, Lucca
This atmospheric antique jewellers, set under frescoed vaults dating from 1800, also sells silver and watches. ⊗ Map C2 • Via Fillungo 95

4 Enoteca Vanni, Lucca
Lucca's best wine shop is guaranteed to raise the hairs on your neck, with its hundreds of bottles crowded into small cellar rooms. ⊗ Map C2 • Piazza Salvatore 7

5 Antico Caffè di Simo, Lucca
Since 1846 this has been the Lucca café of choice for musical and literary luminaries. The interiors are of the period, and the food and pastries are rather fine. ⊗ Map C2 • Via Fillungo 58 • €

6 Forisportam, Lucca
This is another good shop for presents: you'll pay decent prices for highly decorated Renaissance-style ceramics from Montelupo and Deruta. ⊗ Map C2 • Piazza S. Maria Bianca 2

7 Caffè Kosì, Montecatini Alto
Set in a pretty medieval town above Montecatini Terme, this has been a popular café since 1878. Allow sufficient time to sample the dozens of cocktails and exotic fruit *gelati*. ⊗ Map D2 • Piazza G. Giusti 1 • €€

8 La Capannina, Forte dei Marmi
For 70 years La Capannina – part cocktail bar/restaurant and part night spot – has been serving the best beachside refreshments around. ⊗ Map C2 • Viale A. Franceschi • €€

9 Fappani, Viareggio
Try Fappani's delicious homemade sweets with your morning coffee, preferably on the terrace of this café set in the heart of the seaside promenade's shopping district. ⊗ Map C2 • Viale Marconi 1

10 Rossi, Viareggio
Rossi has been in the same family for four generations. They sell elegant pieces from the top names in Italian jewellery design, while their Viale Marconi boutique carries fashionable gold and silver adornments for the younger set. ⊗ Map C2 • Viale Margherita 50/Viale Marconi 16

For more on shopping in Tuscany **See pp122–3 & 136–7**

Price Categories

For a three-course meal for one with a half bottle of wine (or equivalent meal), taxes and extra charges.

€ under €25
€€ €25–€35
€€€ €35–€55
€€€€ €55–€70
€€€€€ over €70

Left **La Mora a Moriano, near Lucca** Right **La Buca di Sant'Antonio, Lucca**

🔟 Where to Eat

1 La Buca di Sant'Antonio, Lucca

The classy but friendly service and superlative food make this Lucca's top restaurant by far. *(See also p72.)* ⊗ *Map C2 • Via della Cervia 3 • 0583 55 881 • Closed Sun pm, Mon • €€€*

2 Da Bruno, Pisa

Expect to pay restaurant prices at this trattoria. Excellent local dishes, such as a thick *zuppa pisana ribollita*. Try the tiramisu sundae. ⊗ *Map C3 • Via Luigi Bianchi 12 • 050 560 818 • Closed Tue • €€€*

3 Romano, Viareggio

The Franceschini family runs one of the best seafood restaurants in Italy. Excellent wine list. ⊗ *Map C2 • Via Mazzini 122 • 0584 31 382 • Closed Mon • €€€€*

4 Da Galileo, Livorno

Delightfully simple restaurant serving local cuisine. Fish dominates the menu – try the seafood fettucine or salt cod cooked with onion Livorno-style. ⊗ *Map C3 • Via della Campana 20 • 0586 889 009 • Closed Wed, Sun pm • €€€*

5 'L Purtunzin d'Ninan, Carrara

Tiny but comfortable wine bar and trattoria, where the chefs have trained with the best in the business. Superb local seafood. ⊗ *Map C2 • Via Bartolini 3 • 0585 74741 • Closed Mon • €€€*

6 Venanzio, Colonnata, near Carrara

Venanzio Vannucci produces his own *lardo di Colonnata* (pork lard in spices) and his recipe is not to be missed. Also try the ravioli with mountain herbs and the guinea fowl with truffles. ⊗ *Map C2 • Piazza Palestro 3 • 0585 758 062 • Closed Thu pm, Sun pm; Christmas–Jan • €€€*

7 Osteria dei Cavalieri, Pisa

A friendly tavern on the ground floor of a medieval tower-house. Try the beans and *funghi* (mushrooms). ⊗ *Map C3 • Via San Frediano 16 • 050 580 858 • Closed Sat L, Sun • €€€*

8 La Mora a Moriano, near Lucca

La Mora serves Lucchese cuisine plus a superb *cacciucco* (fish stew). ⊗ *Map C2 • Via Sesto di Moriano 1748 • 0583 406 402 • Closed Wed • €€€*

9 Da Leo, Lucca

Da Leo is crowded with locals and buzzing with conversation. Try the *zuppa ai cinque cereali*, a soup filled with grains and legumes. ⊗ *Map C2 • Via Tegrimi 1 • 0583 492 236 • € • No credit cards*

Da Leo, Lucca

10 Ghiné e Cambri, Livorno

Located on the coast just outside the town. Excellent seafood. ⊗ *Map C3 • Via di Quercianella 263 • 0586 579 414 • Closed Mon, Tue Oct–May • €€*

Note: Unless otherwise stated, all restaurants accept credit cards and serve vegetarian meals

Left **Church façade, San Gimignano** Centre **Piazza, Massa Marittima** Right **Local pottery**

Western Hill Towns

WHEN PEOPLE IMAGINE *the archetypal Tuscan hill town, they are most likely to be picturing those in the area west of Siena. This is where San Gimignano thrusts its grey stone towers into blue skies, where Volterra's medieval streets and alabaster artisans sit atop "a towering great bluff that gets all the winds and sees all the world" (D. H. Lawrence). More off the beaten track, the underrated Elsa Valley is home to other attractive hill towns, including Colle di Val d'Elsa, Certaldo and Castelfiorentino, which have virtually no crowds and offer a better glimpse of genuine Tuscan town life.*

Western Hill Towns and Sights

1. San Gimignano
2. Volterra
3. Massa Marittima
4. Monteriggioni
5. San Galgano
6. Colle di Val d'Elsa
7. Empoli
8. San Miniato
9. Certaldo
10. Castelfiorentino

Massa Marittima

Piazza della Cisterna, San Gimignano

For more on Tuscan hill towns **See pp56–7**

Alabaster shop, Volterra

San Gimignano
The ultimate hill town ranks second to none among Tuscany's overall Top 10 for its remarkable medieval stone "skyscrapers", fine white wine and gorgeous Gothic frescoes. *(See pp18–19.)*

Volterra
Alabaster-carving is the local speciality of this windswept town with its medieval alleyways. The Museo Etrusco Guarnacci *(see page 48)* has one of Italy's finest Etruscan collections, and the worn basalt heads adorning Porta all'Arco (4th century BC) represent Etruscan gods. The remains of a Roman theatre and baths are best seen from the viewing point off Via Guarnacci. The Pisan-striped 13th-century Duomo, with its meticulously carved and painted ceiling, houses Byzantine and Renaissance treasures, while the Pinacoteca boasts a fully intact Taddeo di Bartolo altarpiece (1411), Ghirlandaio's final painting (*Apotheosis of Christ*, 1492), Luca Signorelli's *Annunciation* (1491) and Rosso Fiorentino's

masterful early Mannerist *Deposition* (1521). ◈ *Map D4*
• Tourist office: via Giusto Turazza, 2
• 0588 861 50 • www.volterra-toscana.net

Massa Marittima
This old mining town has a number of esoteric museums on the subject. Of particular artistic interest are the Dark Ages reliefs decorating the Romanesque Duomo. The Palazzo del Podestà houses a museum containing Ambrogio Lorenzetti's *Maestà* (1330s) and a tiny pre-Etruscan menhir (flat stone carved vaguely as a person). The upper "new town" (developed in the 14th century) is defended by the Gothic Torre del Candeliere and ramparts, offering fine views over the town and Colline Metallifere (literally the "iron-rich hills"). ◈ *Map D4 • Tourist office: Via N Parenti 22 • 0566 902 756*
• www.amatur.it • information booth on Piazza Garibaldi 1 • 0566 902 289

Monteriggioni
The subject of the most popular aerial-shot postcard in Tuscany is a tiny hamlet two streets wide. It is entirely enclosed within medieval walls, whose 14 towers were compared by Dante to the Titans guarding the lowest level of Hell. The town holds a week-long medieval festival in July.
◈ *Map E4 • Tourist office: Largo Fontebranda 5 • 0577 304 810*

Left **Piazza Garibaldi, Massa Marittima** Right **Craft shop, Monteriggioni**

Left **San Galgano** Right **Palazzo Campana, Colle di Val d'Elsa**

San Galgano

This roofless 13th-century abbey and unique domed chapel on the hillside above are associated with the legend of a 12th-century soldier who plunged his sword into a stone to mark the end of his warrior ways. Ambrogio Lorenzetti frescoes (1344) illustrate the holy vision that triggered the incident *(see p29)* Ⓢ Map E4 • Abbazia di S. Galgano • Open 8am–noon, 2pm–sunset • Free

Colle di Val d'Elsa

Enter from the west to pass under Baccio d'Agnolo's Mannerist Palazzo Campana gate (1539). The Duomo features a Giambologna/Pietro Tacca bronze crucifix and, in Mino da Fiesole's tabernacle, a nail said to be from Christ's cross. Palazzo Pretorio's archaeological museum is most interesting for the 1920s political graffiti scrawled on this former prison's inner walls by imprisoned Communists. The (intentionally)

Dante

Dante Alighieri (1265–1321) was Florence's White Guelph (papal) diplomat to San Gimignano. Exiled from Florence on trumped-up charges when the Black Guelphs took over, Dante roamed Italy writing poetry, including the epic *Divine Comedy*. His choice of writing in Tuscan vernacular rather than Latin legitimized and codified the Italian language.

sgraffito-covered façade of Palazzo dei Priori hides a small museum of Sienese paintings. Ⓢ Map E3 • Tourist office: Via Campana 43 • 0577 922 791

Empoli

Piazza Farinata degli Uberti is ringed by 12th- and 13th-century palaces and the Romanesque Sant'Andrea church. Collegiata di Sant'Andrea museum contains a Masolino *Pietà* (1425) and a 1447 font carved by Bernardo Rossellino. Masolino shows up again at

Piazza Farinata, Empoli

Santo Stefano with a large *Madonna and Child* fresco; Rossellino with an *Annunciation*. ✪ Map D3 • Tourist office: Via G. del Papa 98 • 0571 76 115

Duomo, San Miniato

8 San Miniato

Frederick II built the imposing hilltop "Rocca" (great views) when this was the Tuscan stronghold of the German Holy Roman Emperors. The Duomo's (rebuilt) Romanesque brick façade is studded with 13th-century North African majolica bowls. ✪ Map D3 • Tourist office: Piazza del Popolo 1 • 0571 42 745

9 Certaldo

Charming little brick town. Benozzo Gozzoli teamed with Giusto di Andrea on the *Giustiziati* tabernacle in Santi Michele e Jacopo church. Also inside, a 1503 bust and 1954 tombstone commemorate *Decameron* author Boccaccio (1313–75), who may have been born here; the Casa del Boccaccio, in which he passed his final years, is now a small museum and study library.
✪ Map D3 • Tourist info: Viale Fabiani 31 • 0571 656 721

10 Castelfiorentino

Santa Verdiana is Tuscany's loveliest and most successful Baroque church. Its interior is swathed in frescoes celebrating the odd life of Verdiana, who walled herself into a cell here for 34 years with two snakes, which God sent to test her.
✪ Map D3 • Tourist office: Via Ridolfi, at the train station • 0571 629 049 • Closed Nov–Mar

---

Three Towns in a Day

Morning

🕐 Start early in **Monteriggioni** *(see p113)* which takes all of five minutes to walk from one end to the other, but take time to stop in the bar on the piazza for a cappuccino.

Drive on to **Volterra** *(p113)* starting with San Francesco and its amazing frescoes. On the Piazza dei Priori admire the Palazzo dei Priori (1208–57), the oldest Gothic town hall in Tuscany and the model for most others, including Florence's Palazzo Vecchio. Tucked into an alcove on the square is the back door of the Duomo – dive inside. Head down Via dei Sarti for the Pinacoteca; continue on this street, which becomes Via di Sotto, lined with several good alabaster workshops, then Via Don Minzoni, where the Etruscan Museum lies.

Afternoon

One block back, on Piazza XX Settembre, Il Sacco Fiorentino is a good spot for a quick lunch before retrieving your car and continuing to **San Gimignano** *(see pp18–19)* getting there just as the tour buses are leaving (but before 4pm in winter, when things close early). Take a quick spin through the Collegiata frescoes before clambering up the Torre Grossa for perhaps the most beautiful panorama in Tuscany.

If you have time after descending – and after pausing at the Museo Civico – head to the other end of town for Sant'Agostino's frescoes (by 6:30pm). Try to be up on the Rocca for sunset over the towers.

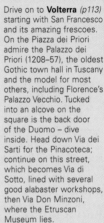

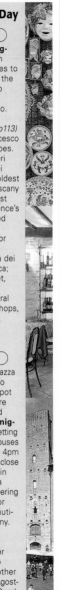

Left **Bar I Combattenti** Centre **Gallerie Agostiniane** Right **L'Incontro**

🔟 Shops and Cafés

1 Bar I Combattenti, San Gimignano

Get great home-made *gelato* and decent coffee on San Gimignano's main street. ✎ *Via S. Giovanni 124 • Map D3 • €*

2 Souvenir Shops, San Gimignano

Tacky souvenir shops line the Via S. Giovanni, selling medieval-style crossbows, swords and flails of varying degrees of realism. Most of them are small and very blunt, but some are fully functional. ✎ *Via S. Giovanni • Map D3*

3 Società Cooperativa Artieri Alabastro, Volterra

Since 1895 this has been the principal outlet for alabaster artisans without a shop of their own. ✎ *Piazza dei Priori 4–5 • Map D4*

4 Gallerie Agostiniane, Volterra

Another showcase for alabaster workers who are too busy to maintain their own sales outlets. ✎ *Piazza XX Settembre 3–5 • Map D4*

5 Enoteca Le Logge, Massa Marittima

This is a great, simple Old World café-bar with tables set under the partly frescoed portico of the main piazza; their sandwiches and *gelato* are definitely worth a try. ✎ *Piazza Garibaldi 11 • Map D4 • €*

6 Enoteca la Botte e il Frantoio, San Gimignano

This retail outlet for Luciano Bruni's Vernaccia wine also sells olive oils and other top wines from across Tuscany. ✎ *Via S. Giovanni 56 • Map D3*

7 L'Incontro, Volterra

This pastry and *panino* wine bar occupies an airy medieval room. Don't miss the deli counter at the back. ✎ *Via Matteoti 18 • Map D4*

8 Belli, Colle di Val d'Elsa

The Etruscans crafted crystal in this area. Belli is the best of those workshops carrying on the tradition, producing both refined objects and souvenirs. ✎ *Via Diaz 10 • Map E3*

Massa Marittima pottery

9 Il Cantuccio di Federigo, San Miniato

The Gazzarrinis have been making superb pastries, cakes and biscuits for five generations. To go with the *cantucci* they carry over 40 *vin santo* labels. ✎ *Via P. Maioli 67 • Map D3*

10 Spartaco Montagnani, Volterra

Visit the shop of this local sculptor who creates original bronzes as well as replicas of works in the museum. ✎ *Via Porta all'Arco 6 • Map D4*

Price Categories

For a three-course meal for one with a half bottle of wine (or equivalent meal), taxes and extra charges.	€ under €25
	€€ €25–€35
	€€€ €35–€55
	€€€€ €55–€70
	€€€€€ over €70

Left **La Mangiatoia** Right **Taverna del Vecchio Borgo**

Where to Eat

1 Dorandò, San Gimignano
Crisp tablecloths and crisp service are coupled with fascinating menus explaining the medieval or Etruscan origins of each finely prepared dish. ⊗ *Vicolo dell'Oro 2 • Map D3 • Tel. 0577 941 862 • Closed Mon Dec–Mar • €€€€*

2 Osteria delle Catene, San Gimignano
Dine in a softly lit brick-barreled vault. Like any good osteria, this one serves great platters of mixed cheeses and cured meats, along with a good selection of wines. ⊗ *Via Mainardi 18 • Map D3 • 0577 941 966 • €€*

3 La Mangiatoia, San Gimignano
The more imaginative dishes at "The Trough" are excellent (though the standard fare seems perfunctorily prepared). Classical music adds to the lively atmosphere. ⊗ *Via Mainardi 5 • Map D3 • 0577 941 528 • €€€*

4 Da Badò, Volterra
This locals' restaurant sticks to its guns: Volterran dishes made only with ingredients available at market that day. ⊗ *Borgo San Lazzero, just outside the walls • Map D4 • 0588 86 477 • €€*

5 Trattoria del Sacco Fiorentino, Volterra
Enjoy seasonal specialities and superb wines at this cosy central trattoria. ⊗ *Piazza XX Settembre • Map D4 • 0588 88 537 • Closed Wed • €€€*

6 Osteria da Tronca, Massa Marittima
A family-run trattoria in a room with stone walls and hewn beams. This is Tuscan cooking the way Grandma used to make it (Grandma, incidentally, *is* in the kitchen). ⊗ *Vicolo Porte 5 • Map D4 • 0566 901 991 • €€*

7 Taverna del Vecchio Borgo, Massa Marittima
Suckling pigs roast on spits in the open fireplace; low stone vaults add to the atmosphere. Try the *tris di primi* sampler plate of three first courses. ⊗ *Via Norma Parenti 12 • Map D4 • 0566 903 950 • €€*

8 Arnolfo, Colle di Val d'Elsa
Sample refined cooking in a 15th-century palazzo. Sample, too, the enormous wine cellar, which ranges from little-known local labels to grand foreign wines. ⊗ *Via XX Settembre 50–52a • Map E3 • 0577 920 549 • €€€€€*

9 Il Vecchio Mulino, Saline di Volterra
Try the hearty *cinghiale alla Volterrana* (wild boar with black olives) in this 19th-century converted mill. ⊗ *Via del Molino • Map D4 • 0588 44 199 • €€€*

10 Le Terrazze, San Gimignano
A fine restaurant with legendary cuisine in the Hotel Cisterna. Stupendous views of the Val d'Elsa and Chianti hills. ⊗ *Piazza della Cisterna 24 • Map D3 • 0577 940 328 • €€€*

Note: *Unless otherwise stated, all restaurants accept credit cards and serve vegetarian meals*

Left **Montepulciano** Centre **Restaurant sign, Pienza** Right **Baths, Montepulciano**

Southern Tuscany

IF EVER BACCHUS BLESSED A LANDSCAPE, *it was the hilly terrain south of Siena. The dry clay soil is ideal for those Mediterranean plants: grape vines and olive trees. Two of Italy's mightiest red wines hail from these parts – Brunello di Montalcino and Vino Nobile di Montepulciano. And where even the vines can't take hold, grasslands thrive to provide rich grazing for sheep on the hills around Pienza, their milk producing the finest* pecorino *cheeses. Medieval hill towns, isolated monasteries, cypress-lined roads, Renaissance palazzi, Sienese School altarpieces and Etruscan tombs complete the picture.*

Left **Rooftops, Montepulciano** Right **Hillside house, Montalcino**

🔟 Sights in Southern Tuscany

1. Montepulciano
2. Pienza
3. Montalcino
4. Sant'Antimo
5. Chiusi
6. Monte Oliveto Maggiore
7. San Quirico d'Orcia
8. Asciano
9. Bagno Vignoni
10. Buonconvento

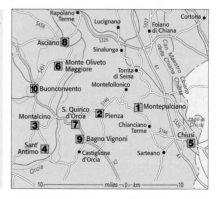

14th-century Fortezza, Montalcino

Montepulciano

Hill town with buildings by major Renaissance architects and Tuscany's second greatest wine, Vino Nobile *(see p63)*. Via Gracciano nel Corso is lined with Renaissance palazzi by the likes of Vignola and Antonio Sangallo the Elder, but also look out for Palazzo Bucelli (no. 73), its base embedded with Etruscan urns.

Piazza Grande is flanked with palaces by Sangallo, the town's Duomo and the Palazzo Comunale, which is Michelozzo's tribute to Florence's Palazzo Vecchio. Inside the Duomo are sculptures by Michelozzo that once formed a single tomb, while the gilded altarpiece is Taddeo di Bartolo's Sienese Gothic masterpiece of 1401.

Set on a patch of grass below the town walls is Sangallo's geometrically precise Tempio di San Biagio (1518–34), the best example of the High Renaissance trend towards Greek Cross churches. ◈ *Map F4 • Tourist info: Piazza Don Minzoni 1 • 0578 757 341 • www.comune.montepulciano.siena.it and www.siena.turismo.toscana.it*

Pienza

In the 15th century, Pope Pius II hired Rossellino to revamp his home village with an assemblage of buildings on the main square, including a retro-Gothic town hall, a palace for the bishop (housing the Museo Diocesano of paintings by Pietro Lorenzetti, Vecchietta and Bartolo di Fredi), a papal palace (great hanging gardens) and a Duomo *(see p47)*. High Street Corso Rossellino is packed with wine and cheese shops. ◈ *Map F4 • Tourist info: Corso Rossellino 59 • 0578 749 071 • www.siena.turismo.toscana.it and www.terresiena.it*

Montalcino

The hometown of Tuscany's mightiest wine, Brunello *(see p63)*, is a small but proud burg, with an excellent wine shop in the ruined 14th-century Fortezza, a split-level main square and a lanky 1292 tower. The Museo Civico e Diocesano houses paintings by Simone Martini, Sano di Pietro and Vecchietta, and polychrome wood statues by Francesco di Valdambrino. ◈ *Map E4 • Tourist info: Via Costa Municipio 1 • 0577 849 331 • www.siena.turismo.toscana.it and www.terresiena.it*

Sant'Antimo

French-style Romanesque abbey church in a beautiful countryside setting *(see p46)*.

Left **View of Pienza** Right **Town square, Pienza**

Left **Piazza, Chiusi** Right **Spa, Bagno Vignoni**

Chiusi

The fine Museo Archeologico Nazionale Etrusco in Chiusi contains *bucchero* (black Etruscan earthenware), bronzes, anthropomorphic canopic jars and even a few 2nd-century BC painted funerary urns. Apply here to visit the best decorated tombs in the valley.

The 12th-century Duomo is swathed in trompe-l'oeil frescoes (1887–94) that look like medieval mosaics. Next door, the Museo della Cattedrale preserves 15th-century illuminated scores from Monte Oliveto Maggiore. Meet here for guided visits to the Etruscan-carved "Labirinto di Porsenna" tunnels. ◈ *Map F5 • Tourist info: Piazza Duomo 1 • 0578 227 667 • www.siena.turismo.toscana.it*

Monte Oliveto Maggiore

Nestled amid a cypress-covered hilltop in the *crete senesi* landscape of eroded clay and limestone bluffs is a 1313 Benedictine monastery. It guards a cloister frescoed with the *Life of St Benedict*, a masterpiece of High Renaissance narrative

Museo Archeologico, Chiusi

Monastic Life

Contemplative Benedictines retreated to isolated countryside monasteries, but Franciscans and Dominicans were preaching orders, and favoured town centres and huge churches to draw the masses (most effective under Dominican Savonarola, *see p78*). Most were scholarly, illuminating manuscripts and using herbal knowledge to run pharmacies so successfully that many are still in business today.

painting by Signorelli (the west wall's eight scenes; 1497–98) and Sodoma (the other 25 scenes; 1505–1508). Sodoma inserted a self-portrait in the third scene, his pet badgers at his feet. ◈ *Map E4 • Monte Oliveto Maggiore • 0577 707 018 • 9:15am–noon, 3:15–5:45pm • Free*

San Quirico d'Orcia

Friendly little farming town with amazing Romanesque carvings on the Collegiata's trio of 12th-century portals: fantastical creatures, stacked arches, tiny telamons and thin columns "knotted" in the centre and resting on toothless lions. Inside is a sumptuous Sano di Pietro altarpiece. ◈ *Map E4 • Tourist info: Via Dante Alighieri 33 • 0577 897 211*

Asciano

Within its 14th-century walls, next to the travertine Romanesque Collegiata, Asciano's Museo d'Arte Sacra

contains Sienese works by Ambrogio Lorenzetti, Segna di Buonaventura and Francesco di Valdambrino. The minuscule Museo Etrusco's 3rd- to 5th-century BC painted vases are installed in a deconsecrated church. ◈ Map E4 • Tourist info: Corso Matteoti 18 • 0577 719 510
• www.siena.turismo.toscana.it

Bagno Vignoni
Little more than a square of houses around a vast, Medici-built portico and basin steaming with naturally carbonated, volcanically heated waters. St Catharine bathed here for her scrofula (lymphatic tuberculosis), Lorenzo the Magnificent for his troublesome arthritis, but sadly the pool is no longer suitable for swimming. ◈ Map E5

Buonconvento
The tiny historic centre shelters a good Museo d'Arte Sacra, with Sienese School works by Duccio, Sano di Pietro and Matteo di Giovanni, who also left a Madonna and Child in the 14th-century Santi Piero e Paolo church. ◈ Map E4 • Tourist info: Via Soccini 18 • 0577 807 181
• www.siena.turismo.toscana.it

Basilica, Asciano

A Day's Drive

Morning

A 9am start in **Chiusi**, at the Museo Archeologico Etrusco. After learning about the Etruscans, head across the piazza to join a Labirinto di Porsenna tour. They leave every half hour, so you might be able to squeeze in a 10-minute tour of the Museo della Cattedrale as well.

Pick up winding S146 to **Montepulciano** (see p119). Park at the base of town to stroll up Via Gracciano nel Corso (its name changes constantly), sampling wines along the way. Since 1858, Liberty-style Caffè Poliziano (Via Voltaio nel Corso 27-29), has served light lunches with countryside views.

Afternoon

Continuing up the main street, pop inside the Gesù for Andrea Pozzo's illusionary painted "dome". Next, it's Piazza Grande (more winery shops) and then on to the Duomo.

En route to **Pienza** (p119) at Montepulciano's edge, turn right (signposted) to see the Tempio di San Biagio (but skip the bare inside). Pienza is a quick stop. After admiring the altarpieces in the **Duomo** (see p47) and giant cracks from the cliff's settlement, tour Pius II's Palazzo Piccolomini. An alley by the palazzo leads to Via Gozzante, a panoramic walkway out of town.

Go on to **Montalcino** (p119). If you're visiting in summer, head to the fortress for sunset views from the ramparts. In winter, make your way to the Caffè Fiaschetteria Italiana in the main square.

Left **Wine shop, Avignonesi** Centre **Biagiotti sign** Right **Osteria Sette di Vino, Pienza**

Wine, Food and Crafts Shops

1 Pulcino, Montepulciano
Loads of free samples of wine, grappa and salamis from the family farm. Atmospheric cellars contain an Etruscan tomb and medieval iron implements thrown into its well long ago. ◈ Map F4 • Via Gracciano nel Corso 102 • 9am–8pm

2 Avignonesi/Classica, Montepulciano
Classy, vaguely medieval showroom and free tasting bar for one of the top wine producers in Tuscany. ◈ Map F4 • Via Gracciano nel Corso 91 • 10am–1pm, 3–7pm

3 La Bottega del Cacio, Pienza
Food boutique selling every kind of *pecorino* cheese along with honey, patés, marmalades and olive oils. ◈ Map F4 • Corso Rossellino 66 • 9:30–1pm, 3–7:30pm

4 Biagiotti & Figli, Pienza
Cast and wrought iron of great beauty in everything from candlesticks to bedsteads and fantastical chandeliers. ◈ Map F4 • Corso Rossellino 67 • 10am–1pm, 3–7:30pm

5 Enoteca La Fortezza, Montalcino
Best selection of wine (and other food products) in town. Gorgeous setting in the airy remains of the medieval fortress. ◈ Map E4 • La Fortezza • Apr–Oct 9am–8pm; Nov–Mar 9am–6pm

6 Aliseda, Montepulciano
Heart-stopping price tags on unique gold jewellery, inspired by ancient museum pieces. ◈ Map F4 • Via dell'Opio nel Corso 8 • 9:30am–8pm (summer closed Sun–Mon)

7 Maledetti Toscani, Montepulciano
A bit of everything hand-crafted and Tuscan: leatherwork, wrought iron, copper pots etc. ◈ Map F4 • Via Voltaia nel Corso 40 • 10am–8pm

8 Bottega del Rame, Montepulciano
The Mazzetti family's beautiful hand-hammered copperware. ◈ Map F4 • Via dell'Opio nel Corso 64 • 9:30am–7:30pm

9 Souvenir Bernardini, Montalcino
Hotchpotch of local crafts, from copper kitchenware to grappa glasses. ◈ Map E4 • Piazzale Fortezza 1 • 10am–8pm (to 6pm in winter)

10 Legatoria Koiné, Montepulciano
Quality leather-bound notebooks. ◈ Map F4 • Via Gracciano nel Corso 22 • 8:30am–1pm, 3:30–7pm

La Solita Zuppa

Price Categories

For a three-course meal for one with half a bottle of wine (or equivalent meal), taxes and extra charges.

€ under €25
€€ €25–€35
€€€ €35–€55
€€€€ €55–€70
€€€€€ over €70

Left **Trattoria Sciame, Montalcino** Right **Ristorante Zaira, Chiusi**

TOP 10 Where to Eat

1 La Chiusa, Montefollonico
Set in an 18th-century mill, La Chiusa won a Michelin star in 2002 for its creative Tuscan cooking. ✎ Map F4 • Via della Madonnina 88 (near Montepulciano/Pienza) • 0577 669 668 • www.ristorantelachiusa.it • Closed Tue • €€€€€

2 Ristorante del Poggio Antico, near Montalcino
Refined restaurant in the converted stalls of a top Brunello vineyard. Home-baked breads and innovative Tuscan cuisine. Booking advised. ✎ Map E4 • Loc. 1 Poggi • 0577 849 200 • Closed Sun pm, Mon & three weeks in Jan • €€€€

3 Ristorante Zaira, Chiusi
Best restaurant in a renowned culinary town. Speciality is *pasta del lucumone* ("Big King's pasta"), a baked casserole of ham and three cheeses. ✎ Map F5 • Via Arunte 12 • 0578 20 260 • Closed Mon (winter) • €€

4 La Solita Zuppa, Chiusi
A cosy restaurant offering southern Tuscan dishes such as *pici* with duck sauce. ✎ Map F5 • Via Porsenna 21 • 0578 21 006 • www.lasolitazuppa.it • Closed Tue; Jan–Feb • €€

5 La Fattoria, Lago di Chiusi
Converted farmhouse/inn by Chiusi's lake, which provides the fresh catch of the day. The *prosciutto* is hand-carved, the pasta homemade and the lake view tranquil. ✎ Map F4 • Via Lago di Chiusi (5km east of Chiusi) • 0578 21 407 • €€

6 Il Cantuccio, Montepulciano
Mid-scale dining in atmospheric rooms, with good, solid Tuscan fare, excellent antipasto and particularly tasty duck dishes. ✎ Map F4 • Via delle Cantine 1–2 • 0578 757 870 • Closed Mon • €€

7 Trattoria Latte di Luna, Pienza
Simple, soulful southern Tuscan cooking *al fresco*. Try the *pici* with garlicky tomatoes or the roast suckling pig. ✎ Map F4 • Via San Carlo 2–4 • 0578 748 606 • Closed Tue • €€

8 Osteria Sette di Vino, Pienza
Tiny osteria with great mixed platters of *pecorino* cheese and salamis and a secret-family-recipe salad dressing. ✎ Map F4 • Piazza di Spagna 1 • 0578 749 092 • €

9 L'Angolo, Montalcino
Tiny, popular trattoria in the town centre, where you can try *pinci* in wild boar sauce and veal with forest-picked asparagus. ✎ Map E4 • Via Ricasoli 9 • 0577 848 017 • €€

10 Fattoria Pulcino, Montepulciano
A rustic experience at long wooden tables – good, simple food in abundance. The family-run wine estate also has a shop where you can buy its farm products and wines. ✎ Map F4 • Via SS146 per Chianciano 37 (3 km/ 2 miles SW of town) • 0578 758 711 • €

Note: Unless otherwise stated, all restaurants accept credit cards and serve vegetarian meals.

Left **Outside dining, Elba** Centre **Cattle, Monti dell'Uccellina** Right **Rooftops, Elba**

The Southern Coast and Maremma

THIS IS TUSCANY'S UNDISCOVERED CORNER, *a largely flat area with some low hills capped by crumbling ancient hill towns such as Pitigliano and Sorano. Its overgrown valleys hide Etruscan tombs, altars and sunken roads (see p126). This was the heart of Etruria, home to important Etruscan cities and a fertile bread-basket. But the conquering Romans were not so adept at maintaining large-scale drainage and irrigation systems, and this agricultural paradise quickly reverted to malaria-breeding swamp. The population dwindled, the ancient cities crumbled and most Tuscan powers left the Maremma alone. It wasn't until 1828 that Grand Duke Leopold I started draining the land again. Today it is Tuscany's least disturbed repository of Etruscan heritage, while also offering beaches, Tuscany's best natural park and the Tyrrhenian islands.*

Beach view, Elba

Sights on the Southern Coast and Maremma

1 Pitigliano
2 Elba
3 Monti dell'Uccellina
4 Monte Argentario
5 Grosseto
6 Sovana
7 Pupolonia
8 Sorano
9 Saturnia
10 Isola del Giglio

Rocky outcrop, Pitigliano

Pitigliano

Etruscan Pitigliano seems to grow right out of its rocky terrain. This hill town's greatest sight is its medieval self, though the Palazzo Orsini castle (a 13th-century structure, enlarged by Giuliano da Sangallo) houses a few modest museums of local Etruscan finds ("Museo Civico Archeologico") and its own rooms ("Palazzo Orsini").
The synagogue offers tours (Wednesday, Friday and Sunday) of Pitigliano's significant Jewish heritage, which all but vanished with Nazi deportations.
⊗ Map F6 • Tourist info: Piazza Garibaldi 51 • 0564 617 111
• www.lamaremmafabene.it

Elba

This modestly scaled resort island derives its name from *Aethalia*, the Greek word for the sparks of its busy iron forges. Portoferraio, where ferries arrive

Portoferraio, Elba

from Piombino, has two fortress/parks, Napoleon's Villa dei Mulini (his Villa San Martino south of town is more interesting, however), and a small archaeological museum. Porto Azzuro was the island's Spanish capital and is today a bustling resort that manages to retain something of the old fishing town. Hilltop Capoliveri has the best nightlife and evocative medieval alleyways. Ancient Marciana is a good hill town base for exploring the island's western half *(see p69)*.
⊗ Map C5 • Tourist info: Calata Italia 26, Portoferraio • 0565 914 671
• www.arcipelago.turismo.toscana.it

Monti dell'Uccellina

Tuscany's greatest protected parkland. Coastal Monti dell' Uccellina ("Mountains of the Little Bird") is a large area of pine forests, teeming with boar, roe deer and porcupines, bird-filled marshland to the north, as well as tracts of pristine beach. A pack of wild horses and roaming long-horned white Maremma cattle are looked after by Butteri cowboys. Buses from Albarese take you to the park's centre. ⊗ Map E6 • Park entrance at Albarese • 0564 407 098 • 7am–dusk (9am–dusk Oct–14 Jun) • Admission charge
• www.parco–maremma.it

Monte Argentario

This quietly chic and beautiful peninsula is really an almost-circular island, connected to the Tuscan mainland by causeways *(see p69)*. ⊗ Map E6
• Tourist info: Corso Umberto 55, Porto Santo Stefano • 0564 814 208
• www.lamaremmafabene.it

Left **Busy street, Grosseto** Right **Pupolonia tomb**

Grosseto

Grubby Grosseto lacks real charm, but its Museo Civico Archeologico e d'Arte della Maremma is a must for Etruscan lovers. Many of the more portable finds from the Maremma are housed here, along with works of art from city churches, including Guido da Siena's 13th-century *Last Judgement* and a Sassetta *Madonna of the Cherries*. The 13th-century church of San Francesco has fresco fragments and a high altar *Crucifix* (1285) attributed to Duccio. ❧ *Map E5 • Tourist info: Via Monterosa, 206 • 0564 462 611 • www.lamaremmafabene.it*

Sovana

This modest hamlet was once an Etruscan city, Roman *Municipium*, and birthplace of 11th-century Aldobrandeschi Pope Gregory "Hildebrand" VII, who reigned for 60 years. On the main square are a medieval Palazzo Pretorio and Santa Maria church, which contains

The Vie Cave

No one is sure why the Etruscans dug these "sunken roads", narrow canyons up to 20 m (65 ft) deep into the Maremma's rocky ground. Many extend for miles between settlements. They may have been defensive, religious (some led to tombs or altars), for herding or perhaps some mixture of all these possibilities.

15th-century frescoes and a rare 9th-century altar canopy. The Duomo on the edge of town preserves carvings from the Dark Ages. The surrounding hills and valley are littered with signposted Etruscan tombs, altars and *vie cave (see box)*; the best is the Tomba Ildebranda. ❧ *Map F6*

Populonia

Baratti Bay's Iron Age role as port for Elba's mines helped preserve Populonia's Etruscan necropolis – under a slag heap. Half a dozen of the tombs are visitable, several almost intact. Museo Gasparri has many of the items excavated here. ❧ *Map C5 • Baratti • 0565 29 002 • Necropolis open Mar–May, Oct: 10am–6pm Tue–Sun; Jul, Aug: 10am–7pm daily; Jun, Sep: 10am–7pm Tue–Sun; Nov–Feb: 10am–4pm Sat–Sun • www. parchivaldicornia.it • Admission charge*

Sovana's medieval square

Etruscan tomb, Sovana

8 Sorano

Sorano is an ancient Etruscan hill town literally slipping off its rocky outcrop. The restored 13th-century Aldobrandeschi fortress (expanded by the Orisini in 1552), is now partly medieval museum and partly hotel *(see p142)*. The 18th-century Massa Leopoldino fortress is also open to visitors. ✆ *Map F5 • Tourist info: Piazza Busati • 0564 633 099 • www.comune.sorano.gr.it*

9 Saturnia

You come to Saturnia, not for the little town and its 15th-century Sienese castle, but to take the waters. The warm, mineral-rich waters in the valley feed both a four-star spa (which is elegant, but smells of rotten eggs), hotel complex and a lovely outdoor stream (Cascate del Gorello), which gushes down a hillside, running into small pools and waterfalls. *(See pp68–9.)* ✆ *Map E6*

10 Isola del Giglio

This hilly isle off l'Argentario (ferries from Porto Santo Stefano) has a medieval hamlet Castello above the docks, a beach at the port and an even better low-key resort and beach on the bay at Campese. Ansonico, the local wine, is known mainly to the habitués who crowd here on summer weekends. ✆ *Map D6 • Tourist info: Via Provinciale 9 • 0564 809 400 • www.isoladelgiglio.it*

The Best of the Maremma in a Day

Morning

🕐 Start in the most dramatic of Maremma's hill towns, **Pitigliano** *(see p125)*, perusing the ultra-modern archaeological museum set in a fortified palazzo.

Head north to **Sorano** to visit the Fortezza degli Orsini (be there by 11am for a tour of its cellars), then poke around the abandoned, cliffside Via delle Rovine neighbourhood.

Ask at the Fortezza for a map of the Etruscan tombs and *vie cave* in the area, then take off towards Sovana, looking out for signs indicating Etruscan ruins *(tomba, ippogeo, via cava)*. Explore as many as you can before heading into **Sovana** for lunch.

Afternoon

Pop into Santa Maria Church and the 11th- to 13th-century Duomo, which preserves good carvings, some of which pre-date the Romanesque.

Follow the twisting road west through San Martino sul Fiora (more Etruscan roadside stops), then turn south to **Saturnia**. Skip the spa and head to the Cascate del Gorello open-air hot springs south of town to wallow in the natural whirlpools.

Go south to Manciano, from where you can reach coastal A12 highway: south to Tarquínia and Cerveteri (for great Etruscan tombs); or north to **Monti dell' Uccellina** *(see p125)*, the Etruscan Riviera beaches, or Piombino and ferries to **Elba** *(see p125)*.

Left **Watersports shop** Centre **Beach view, Elba** Right **La Barca, Elba**

Leisure Activities

1 Parco Naturale della Maremma and Monti dell'Uccellina Trails

"Strada degli Olivi" beelines for the beach. Trail 1 (7.2 km) clambers around San Rabano abbey's ruins. Trail 2 (6 km) passes medieval towers to the rocky south shores. Trail 3 (9.6 km) meanders amid prehistoric caves. Trail 4 (12 km) wanders everywhere. Trails 3 and 4 are occasionally closed (Jun–Sep). ◎ *Map E5 • Admission charge*

2 Exploring Etruscan Tombs around Sovana

Pick up a map in town or at Sorano's fortress, to explore the tombs and *vie cave* hidden in the countryside. ◎ *Map F6*

3 Saturnia's Hot Springs

See pages 68–9 for the best spas and free springs. ◎ *Map E6*

4 Elba's Beaches

Portoferraio may be bland, but boats can whisk you to secluded beaches on the northeast shore. The western coast has rocky shoals (good for snorkelling) and, south of Fetovaia, sandy beaches on tiny inlets. ◎ *Map C5*

Hiking trail sign

5 Scuba and Snorkelling on Elba

Basic lessons and full courses, equipment rental and guided day and night dives. ◎ *Map C5 • Elba Diving Centre, Viale Aldo Moro Marciana Marina • 0565 904256 • www.elbadiving.it*

6 Sailing and Windsurfing on Elba

Rent sailboards, catamarans and Zodiacs, or take windsurfing and sailing courses. ◎ *Map C5 • Aloha • Spiaggia di Lido, Capoliveri • 0368 521 714*

7 Horseback Riding on the Coast

Guided rides from an Orbetello lagoon base. Moonlit rides June to September. ◎ *Map E6 • Il Barbazzale di Amalfitano, Via Aurelia 146, Orbetello Scalo • 0564 864 208*

8 Hiking on Elba

Tourist office brochures lay out a dozen hikes from 90 mins to all day. The most rewarding is up (or down; you may ride the cable car one way) the Monte Capenne, past Sanctuario di San Cerbone church. ◎ *Map C5*

9 Scuba around Monte Argentario

Equipment rentals, lessons, guided dives and snorkelling around l'Argentario and Giglio and Giannutri islands. ◎ *Map E6 • Pelagos Diving Centre, Lungomare A. Doria 11–13, Porto Ercole • 0564 834 200 • www.pelagosdc.com*

10 Etruscan Coast Beaches

The "Etruscan Coast" situated to the south of Livorno includes pine-shaded, sandy, semi-secluded Marina di Albarese and the sandy resort of San Vincenzo. ◎ *Map C3*

Price Categories

For a three-course meal for one with a half bottle of wine (or equivalent meal), taxes and extra charges.

€ under €25
€€ €25–€35
€€€ €35–€55
€€€€ €55–€70
€€€€€ over €70

Left **Alfresco dining** Right **La Canocchia**

🔟 Where to Eat

1 Gambero Rosso, San Vicenzo

One of Italy's top restaurants, with an elegant, blue-and-white Neo-Classical dining room and a menu rich in seafood *(see p72)*. 🗺 *Map C4 • Piazza della Vittoria 13 • 0565 701 021 • Closed Nov, Dec • €€€€€*

2 Da Caino, Montemerano

A rustic-but-elegant room in the Maremma. The highly regarded cooking is inspired by regional cuisine and seasonal ingredients. Bread and pasta are homemade; the wine list is vast. 🗺 *Map E6 • Via Chiesa 4 • 0564 602 817 • Closed Wed • €€€€€*

3 Emanuele, Elba

Unassuming beachfront shack serving Elba's best seafood, freshest vegetables and excellent desserts. The tiny courtyard at the back leads onto the pebble beach. 🗺 *Map C5 • Loc. Enfola, near Portoferraio • 0565 939 003 • €€€*

4 Il Tufo Allegro, Pitigliano

A young-spirited place, where Domenico adds creative touches to local ingredients and Valeria suggests pairings accompanying wines. 🗺 *Map F6 • Vicolo della Constituzione 5 • 0564 616 192 • Closed Tue, Wed L • €€*

5 Osteria del Noce, Elba

The softly lit rustic dining room has a pergola-shaded terrace with sea views. The owners' native Liguria is evident in the cooking. 🗺 *Map C5 • Via della Madonna 14, Marciana • 0565 901 284 • €€€*

6 Osteria del Buco, Castiglione della Pescaia

Small cellar osteria in this fishing village/resort. The Maremmana food is excellent, balancing meat and seafood, and the gregarious owner carries a good tune. 🗺 *Map D5 • Via del Recinto 11 • 0564 934 460 • €€*

7 La Barca, Elba

The best dining room in Portoferraio, one street up from the harbourside quay, with a plant-enclosed awning to catch the breezes. Enjoy typical Elban dishes such as *spaghetti alla bottarga* (with dried tuna roe). 🗺 *Map C5 • Via Guerrazzi 60–62, Portoferraio • 0565 918 036 • €€*

8 Ristorante dei Merli, Sovana

The Merli family's restaurant just off the main square serves tasty Maremmana cooking with a personal touch *(see p144)*. 🗺 *Map F6 • Via R. Siviero 1–3 • 0564 616 531 • €€*

9 La Canocchia, Elba

Close by the sea, this simple restaurant specializes in perfectly prepared seafood. 🗺 *Map C5 • Via Palestro 2/4, Rio Marina • 0565 962 432 • €€*

10 La Taverna Etrusca, Sovana

Pretty good Tuscan cuisine in a room of beamed ceilings and stone archways dating back to the 1200s. 🗺 *Map F6 • Piazza del Pretorio 16 • 0564 616 183 • €€*

Following pages **Bread shop, Lucca**

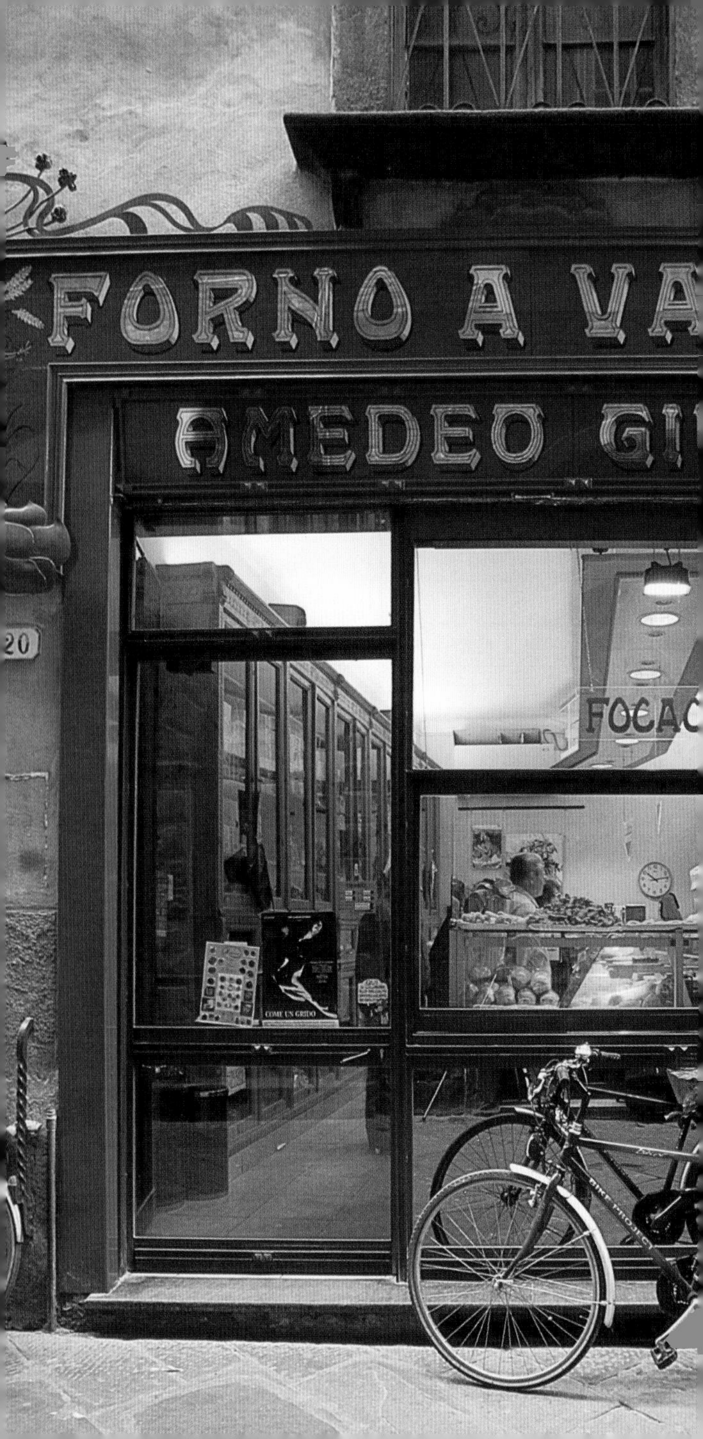
FORNO A VA
AMEDEO GI
20
FOCAC
COME UN GRIDO

STREETSMART

TUSCANY'S TOP 10

Left **Tourist office** Left centre **Tourists, Florence** Right centre **Internet facility** Right **Policemen**

TOP 10 General Information

1 Italian State Tourism Board

ENIT (Ente Nazionale Italiano per il Turismo) is Italy's state tourism board and provides basic information for people planning to visit the country. However, provincial tourism boards are better for more detailed information.

2 Tourist Offices in Tuscany

Local *informazioni turistiche* offices (indicated as "APT" or "Pro Loco") are good for free maps, sight opening hours and hotel directories. The amount of information beyond that varies widely, but most are friendly.

3 Immigration Laws

Citizens of the EU, US, Canada, Australia and New Zealand need only a valid passport to visit Italy for up to 90 days as tourists. A visa is needed for non-EU citizens who are planning to stay more than three months. All visitors to Italy should by law register with the police within three days of arrival. Most hotels will register visitors when they check in.

4 Customs

For travellers entering Italy from outside the EU, limits on personal items are as follows: 200 cigarettes (or 250g of tobacco), one litre of alcohol or two litres of wine. Special permits are required to import guns.

5 Opening Hours

Most shops and businesses open at 8 or 9am, shut for *riposo* from 12:30 or 1pm to 3 or 4pm (museums and churches, too), and close around 6 to 8pm. In larger cities the *riposo* is disappearing in favour of *orario continuato* – "straight through".

6 Electricity & Outlets

Italy is on 220V/50 cycles. To operate a 110V device you need a converter (most laptops and camcorders have this built in). To plug it in, you need an adapter from your pronged plugs to continental Europe's two round pins.

7 TV & Newspapers

Most hotels 3-stars and above get satellite TV with CNN and BBC news. Train station and central piazza newsstands are best for finding English-language magazines and newspapers - *International Herald Tribune* (with an *Italy Daily* insert), *USA Today*, *The Times* (London) and *New York Times*.

8 When to Go

Tuscany has a mild climate, although the August heat can be oppressive, and snow is common in January. Spring's middle ground keeps hotels booked, but autumn, when grapes (September) and olives (October) are harvested and boar and truffles hunted, is the true Tuscan time of year.

9 High Seasons and Holidays

High season in Tuscany runs through from Easter to October. Hotels in Florence are booked solid for Easter, and the beach resorts are packed in July and August. Cities, by contrast, are deserted from 15 to 31 August. The traditional "shoulder seasons" – Tuscany's most crowded times – are mid-September to mid-October and late April and May. National holidays include 1 and 6 January, Easter Sunday and Monday, 25 April, 1 May, 2 June, 15 August, 1 November and 8, 25 and 26 December.

10 What to Pack

The Italians dress well – maybe not always Armani, but usually stylish. Bring one nice outfit. Few restaurants require jacket and tie. Many churches do not allow you to enter with bare knees or shoulders (no shorts, miniskirts, singlets or tank tops); a light shawl around the waist or shoulders solves it.

Directory

ENIT
www.enit.it

Tuscany Regional Tourist Information (APT)
Via Cavour 1, Florence
• 055 290 832 •
www.turismo.toscana.it

Left **Florence's Amerigo Vespucci airport** Centre **Train, Pisa** Right **Ferry, Livorno**

🔟 Arriving in Tuscany

1 By Air from North America
You cannot fly direct to Tuscany, but Alitalia, Continental and Delta can connect you through Rome or Milan to Florence or Pisa.

2 By Air from the UK
British Airways, EasyJet and Ryanair fly London to Pisa. Meridiana and Alitalia fly direct from London to Florence. Also, Easyjet flies to Rome and Bologna, and BMI (British Midland) flies to Rome, Venice and Milan. From Ireland, it's best to go via London, though Ryanair flies from Dublin to Pisa and Aer Lingus flies to Milan and Rome.

3 By Air from Australasia
Cathay-Pacific handles flights from Australia and New Zealand to Italy, in partnership with Qantas, via Hong Kong. There are usually more flights, and it's cheaper, to fly to London first, then Italy.

4 By Air from the Continent
There are flights to Rome from most European capitals; Air France also flies from Paris to Florence, Lufthansa from Munich and Frankfurt to Florence, SN Brussels from Brussels to Florence. Ryanair also flies to Pisa from other European cities.

5 Internet Bargains
Most airlines are now using their own websites to promote sales, last-minute deals, and web-only fares. Expedia and Travelocity collate best fares on offer from the US, UK or Canada.

6 Pisa's Airport
Tuscany's biggest international airport is Pisa's Galileo Galilei. Regular trains and buses take only five minutes into Pisa; shuttle trains and a regular coach service to Florence about an hour.

7 Florence's Airport
Florence's small Aeroporto Amerigo Vespucci/Peretola is served by Volainbus, a shuttle connecting to Florence's main train station every 30 minutes. Tickets may be bought from the driver.

8 By Train
From London, you can take the Eurostar to Paris and pick up a train to Florence, Pisa or Milan. Trains into Tuscany range from express EC/IC/EN (all require high-speed supplements), through speedy IR, to the slow *diretto* and *espresso*. Most international lines stop only at Florence. Make sure you get off at Firenze-Santa Maria Novella. Some coastal trains from France stop at Pisa.

9 Florence's Santa Maria Novella Station
Tourist information and hotel bookings are across from track *(binario)* 5 and train information is opposite the end of track 5. Left luggage is next to track 16. Exit past the end of track 16 for the underground passage that avoids the traffic outside and leads to the centre.

10 By Car
Italy's main motorway, the A1 autostrada, comes from Milan and the north through Bologna to Florence, then down to Rome. The A12 skirts the west coast from Genova (where it links to the A10 from France) down through Pisa, Grosseto, and the Maremma, ending near Rome's Fiumicino airport.

Directory

Airlines
www.airfrance.com
www.alitalia.it www.
britishairways.com
www.cathaypacific.com
www.continental.com
www.delta.com www.
easyjet.com www.
flybmi.com www.flysn.
com www.meridiana.it
www.ryanair.com

Internet Agents
www.lastminute.com
www.expedia.com
www.travelocity.com

Pisa Airport
3 km (2 miles) S of Pisa
• 050 849 300/849 111
• www.pisa-airport.com

Florence Airport
5 km (3 miles) NE of
Florence • 055 306 1300
• www.aeroporto.
firenze.it

Left **Local coach** Left centre **Car rental office** Right centre **Toll booths** Right **Taxi**

Getting Around

1 By Train

Italian trains, run by FS, are speedy and efficient, but don't cover every Tuscan corner. Each station posts its own schedule – departures on yellow, arrivals on white – and newsstands sell national schedules. Ticket queues can be long (automated machines are now helping), and strikes (*sciopero*) frequent. Stamp one end of your ticket at the station's or track's yellow box (or risk a €50 fine).

2 By Coach

Coaches (*pullman*) can be slower and no cheaper than trains; use them to reach towns inaccessible by train.

3 By Rental Car

The best way to explore Tuscany's back roads, hill towns and vineyards. Local outfits are rarely cheaper than international companies, and arranging a rental from your home country is invariably cheaper.

4 Road Maps & Signs

TCI (Touring Club Italiano) maps are best, widely available in Italy but infrequently outside it. Michelin maps have more sightseeing indications, including scenic roads highlighted in green. Italian road signs (green for routing via Autostrada highways, blue for state roads) indicate destinations (albeit inconsistently) more often than route numbers. Always know the name of the first village and major town or city along any road you wish to take.

5 Road Rules

Largely ignored, speed limits are 30–50 kmph (20–30 mph) in town, 80–110 kmph (50–70 mph) on two-lane roads, and 130 kmph (80 mph) on highways. Left lanes are for passing, but on wide enough, hard-shouldered roads, Italians regularly pass by swerving into the oncoming traffic, which obliges by using its own hard shoulder.

6 Tolls and Fuel

Tuscany's only toll roads are the A1 autostrada and the Florence-Pisa A13. Petrol is very expensive. Diesel is widely available. Most filling stations close on Sundays, but even when closed have automated machines that accept notes and, increasingly, credit cards.

7 Parking

Few hotels have their own parking facilities, though many have deals with local garages. A round blue sign with a red slash means no parking. Legal parking is always marked: white-lined spaces are free (though often restricted to residents), yellow spaces off-limits, blue spaces available for an hourly fee, which you pre-pay at a nearby machine (display the ticket it dispenses on your dashboard), or with a scratch-off card, available at tobacconists' (*tabacchi,* indicated by a white-on-brown "T" sign).

8 City Buses

Buy tickets at tobacconists', bars or newsstands. Stamp one end on the bus (*autobus*) when you board. Most are good for a set time period during which you may transfer buses.

9 Taxis

Taxis have ranks at airports and stations. Any hotel or restaurant will call you a taxi. Standard rates go up with luggage, after 8pm, on Sundays and for trips outside the city centre. Tip about 10%.

10 On Foot

No historic centre in Tuscany, Florence included, takes more than 20 to 30 minutes to cross on foot. Many streets are cobblestoned, however, so wear sturdy, comfortable shoes.

Directory

Trains
www.trenitalia.com
• 892 021

Car Rental
www.europebycar.com
www.autoeurope.com

Left **Road signs** Centre **Guided tour party** Left **Cycling in the Chianti**

ⁱ⁰ Specialist Tours

1 Packaged Tours
Airlines and tour companies offer discount packages combining travel and accommodation. Many, though, stick to large international hotel chains, usually on the periphery of town. You get a discount rate, but frequently, better deals can be found at hotels in town and city centres.

2 Standard Guided Tours
Tours make life easy when travelling in Italy – getting round language barriers and transport complications – but they often suck out much of the fun of travel in the process. You see the tour company's idea of Tuscany, not the Tuscany of chance and adventure.

3 Study Vacations
All manner of study vacations are run in Tuscany. For a flavour of what's on offer, check out the websites listed in the directory.

4 Tuscany By Bike
Tuscany offers terrain both tough enough for die-hard peddallers and easy enough for dilettantes who want to experience the details of this beautiful landscape at a leisurely pace. Ciclismo Classico and Experience Plus offer a range of guided and self-guided bike trips, and I Bike Italy does single-day trips around Florence.

5 Cooking Schools
Learn to make *ribollita* soup, stuffed pastas and the perfect *bistecca* (beef steak) in the kitchens of Tuscan chefs. The top schools in the Chianti are run by cookbook diva Lorenza de' Medici at Badia a Coltibuono and Italian TV chef Giuliano Bugialli.

6 Tuscany on Horseback
There is no more romantic way to see Tuscany at a pleasingly slow pace than in the saddle. For horse riding in the Maremma, in northern Tuscany and the Chianti, try Equitour or Il Paretaio.

7 Italian Lessons
Immerse yourself in the language as well as the sights. The best schools are in Florence. (The British Institute and ABC Centro di Lingua e Cultura Italian both offer short courses.) Siena, where many say the most perfect Italian is spoken, has the Centro Internazionale Dante Alighieri. Local tourist boards can help you find courses and tutors in other towns.

8 Art Lessons
Tuscany is awash with artistic example and inspiration. And New York's prestigious School of the Visual Arts – which runs summer courses in Tuscany – could aid your personal renaissance.

9 Brief On-Site Tours
Many churches and museums offer guided tours – some are free, others not. Many towns now also have self-guided walking tours, using rented electronic hand-held guides. Ask at the local tourist office.

10 Private Guides
Local tourist offices keep lists of officially licensed guides available for hire. Rates vary widely; expect to pay at least €9–12 per hour.

Directory

Study Vacations
www.specialtytravel.com
www.shawguides.com
www.infohub.com

Bike Trips
www.ciclismoclassico.com
www.experienceplus.com
www.ibikeitaly.com

Cooking Schools
Lorenza de' Medici
• 0577 74 481
www.coltibuono.com

Giuliano Bugialli
www.bugialli.com

Horse Riding
Equitour
• 800/545 0019 (USA)
www.ridingtours.com

Il Paretaio
• 055 805 9218
www.ilparetaio.it

Art Lessons
www.schoolofvisualarts.edu

Left **Shop front** Centre left **Designer gear** Centre right **Plate** Right **Leather goods**

🔟 Shopping Tips

1 Shop Hours
Shop hours are roughly 8am–8pm with a long lunch break (see p132).

2 Haggling
Expected in markets, much less so in shops. Many market stallholders hail from Middle Eastern countries where bargaining is an art form. The full ritual involves you acting less and less interested, while the stallholder acts more and more offended. Any price agreed upon is good – the stallholder will always make a profit.

3 Tax Refunds
Italy's sales tax (IVA) is incorporated into the price tag of every item. If you spend more than €155 in a shop, you can get the tax refunded. Ask the store to help you fill out the forms; then bring all such forms and the receipts to the customs office at the airport of the last EU country you'll be visiting to complete the paperwork. Your refund will be mailed (though it may take months). Stores marked "Tax Free Shopping for Tourists" speed up the process.

4 Customs Limits
UK and Irish citizens can bring home virtually anything duty free (though theoretical amounts such as 90 litres of wine apply). US citizens are limited to $400-worth of goods duty-free, including 1 litre of alcohol, 200 cigarettes, and 100 cigars. Canadian, Australian and New Zealand limitations are roughly similar. Except to the British Isles, you may not bring home flowers, bulbs, fruits, vegetables, meats (unless tinned), or cheeses runnier than a brie.

5 Leather
Tuscany, especially Florence, is home to some of the world's great leather workers, making jackets, bags, shoes, wallets and belts. From the stalls of San Lorenzo market to the boutiques of Ferragamo and Gucci and the leather school in Santa Croce church, you can find something fetching to fit your budget.

6 Fashion
Tuscany contains the houses of Gucci, Pucci and Ferragamo. There are Gucci and Prada outlet stores (see pp96 & 104), and lesser-known classy local fashion boutiques such as Florence's Madova gloves or Sonia Fortuna clothing. High fashion is rarely cheaper than in other countries, but there is the cachet of having found those great shoes in Florence.

7 Ceramics
Italy is renowned for its hand-painted ceramics. Tuscany's pottery tradition is among the best in Italy. You can find everything from Richard Ginori porcelain and high-class Rampini designs (see p96) to traditional rustic patterns in Montepulciano, Siena and Cortona, and the more prosaic terracotta production in Impruneta.

8 Design Objects
Italians are masters of industrial design, from Ferraris to funky Alessi tea kettles. If the Ferrari doesn't fit your budget, consider shopping for elegant, quirky kitchen implements, homewares, or post-modern lighting systems, many sketched out by today's top international designers on behalf of Italian firms.

9 Crafts & Paper Products
Florentines are masters of the craft of marbled paper, creating intricate, colourful designs by swirling oil-based inks on the surface of a water pan then dipping the paper. They sell it as wrapping paper, and bookbinders sheathe hand-bound books in it. Stationery shops also cover rough-papered journals with leather, sold alongside simple, old-fashioned fountain pens and calligraphy sets.

10 Wine
Tuscany's wine is its best souvenir – though heavy. Shipping is expensive, so save it for when you discover a small vineyard whose wines aren't exported and you want a whole case.

Left **Market toys** Centre **Fine wines** Right **Camper vans**

🔟 Tuscany on a Budget

1 Sightseeing for Free
Churches are usually free, except San Gimignano's Collegiata, Pisa's Duomo and Florence's Santa Maria Novella and Santa Croce. However, you often pay for entry into the best chapels. The piazzas are free theatres of life; for the (steep) price of a cappuccino you can have a front-row seat at a café table. Medieval alleyways and the vine- and olive-clad slopes around them are a joy to wander.

2 Sightseeing at a Discount
Sights and museums are run by a variety of agencies, so discounts or free admissions vary. The age cut-off may be 6, 12, 14, or 18, or just students and seniors over 60 or 65. National museums are free to everyone under 18 and over 60 unless you are American (relating to reciprocity agreements). Many towns now sell cumulative tickets covering several sights.

3 Travel Discounts
Those under 26 can buy a Carta Verde for a 20% discount on any train ticket; for the over 60s, this is called Carta Argento.

4 Lease a Car
For periods longer than 21 days, a short-term lease is often cheaper than renting a car. Unlike with rentals, you also get full insurance coverage with no deductable, plus a brand-new car straight from the factory.

5 Save Money on Accommodation
Prices are often higher towards the centre of town and the more stars to the hotel rating. Making do with a one- or two-star hotel (fewer amenities) is preferable to looking outside the centre or in the uninteresting train station neighbourhoods where cheap hotels congregate. Avoid, if possible, the continental breakfast, the minibar and making phone calls: all are overpriced.

6 Cheap Eats
In food-loving Italy, price or category of restaurant has little to do with how good the food is, so a cheaper osteria or trattoria can be just as tasty as a fancy ristorante. Appetizers tend to cost almost as much as first courses for much less food. House wine is cheaper than bottled; tap water (acqua dal rubinetto) is usually free. Tavole calde and bars offer cheap and quick hot meals.

7 Have a Picnic
Assemble a picnic fit for an Etruscan king from the small delicatessens (alimentari), greengrocers (fruttivendolo), bread and pastry shops (panetteria or pasticceria) and wine stores (enoteca or fiaschetteria).

8 Pay in Cash
Cash will often secure you a discount in shops and smaller hotels. Sometimes they're just passing on to you the savings on the credit card commission. Other times, especially in shops, they're avoiding putting the income on their books. Just make sure you leave with some kind of receipt (by law you have to carry it 400 m beyond the store).

9 Visit in Off-Season
Spring and autumn are becoming more crowded than summer, and hotels and airlines are often extending their high-season prices accordingly. Roughly mid-October to before Easter, though, is low season in Tuscany, when rates on air fares and hotels drop. However, the coastal and spa destinations tend to shut down in winter.

10 Shop Wisely
Some fashion items are no cheaper in Italy than abroad. This is especially true of Made in Italy shoes, but Tuscany's traditional cobblers will make you relatively inexpensive shoes to order. When possible, save your purchasing for one store so you can hurdle the limit for a sales tax refund (see opposite). Seek out artisan products from the craftspeople themselves.

Left **Siena restaurant** Centre left **Studying the menu** Centre right **Plate setting** Right **Waiter**

TOP 10 Dining in Tuscany

1 Restaurant Types

Traditionally, a ristorante is the most formal, and expensive, eatery; a trattoria a family-run, moderately-priced joint; an osteria anything from a simple trattoria to the equivalent of a pub with a few dishes or platters of mixed meats and cheeses along with wine.

2 The Italian Meal

Italian meals, especially dinners, are drawn-out affairs of two to four hours, with the courses listed below followed by an espresso and digestive liqueur *(digestivo)* such as *grappa*. Breakfast is traditionally just an espresso or cappuccino with a croissant.

3 Antipasto

The appetizer course is most traditionally *crostini (see p64)* and/or cured meats such as *prosciutto* and various salami. Also popular are *panzanella*, a summery salad of stale bread soaked in water and olive oil with tomatoes and garlic, and a *caprese* salad of tomatoes and fresh mozzarella.

4 Primo

The first course might be pasta, such as *pappardelle alla lepre* (with hare) or *al cinghiale (see p64)*, *pici* (hand-rolled spaghetti) and *gnocchi* (dumplings of ricotta and spinach, or potato). Soups *(minestre)* include *ribollita (see p64)*,

pappa al pomodoro (tomato and bread pap), and *zuppa di farro* (emmer wheat). Risotto is made with seasonal vegetables.

5 Secondo

The main course. Meats include *bistecca* or *manzo* (beef), *vitello* (veal), *agnello* (mutton), *pollo* (chicken), *maiale* (pork), *cinghiale* (boar), *coniglio* (rabbit) and *anatra* (duck). They are usually simply grilled or roasted. A *grigliata mista* is a hearty mixed meat platter. Fish include *branzino* (bass), *acciughe* (anchovies), *baccalà* (cod), *orata* (bream), *rombo* (turbot), and *sogliola* (sole), usually grilled, roasted or *all'acqua pazza* (simmered in white wine and tomatoes).

6 Dolce

The sweet. Most popular are simple *cantucci e vin santo (see p65)*, though milk *(panna cotta, latte portughese)* and egg (crème caramel) custards are popular, as is the tiramisù trifle and *torta della nonna (p65)*. The lighter *macedonia* is a diced fresh fruit cup.

7 Wine

No Italian meal is complete without red *(rosso)* or white *(bianco)* wine *(vino)*. Try a carafe *(un litro)* or a half-carafe *(mezzo litro)* of the usually excellent house wine *(vino della casa)*, or a bottle of Chianti, Brunello,

Vino Nobile, Vernaccia or other fine Tuscan label *(see pp62–3)*. Italians temper their wine intake with equal amounts of water, either fizzy *(gassata, frizzante)* or still *(non-gassata or naturale)*.

8 Cover Charges and Tipping

The *pane e coperto* cover charge is unavoidable. If the menu says *"servizio incluso"* (or the waiter confirms so when you ask *"E' incluso il servizio?"*), service charge is built in, but it is still customary to round up the total. If it is not included, tip a discretionary 10–15 percent.

9 Restaurant Etiquette

Jacket and tie are rarely required. Service ranges from heartily chummy to restrained, but is usually professional. Waiters expect you to linger over your meal and won't rush you (some tourists mistake this for slow service).

10 Bars and Tavole Calde

Most Italian bars – something between a pub and a café – serve morning cappuccino, espresso pick-me-ups throughout the day, and aperitifs *(aperitivi)* in the evening usually along with simple sandwiches *(panini)*, pastries, and ice cream *(gelato)*. A tavola calda is a glorified bar with dishes steaming in trays behind a glass counter.

For more on traditional Tuscan dishes **See pp64–5**

Left **Hotel façade** Centre **Sign for wine route** Right **View from a balcony**

🔟 Accommodation Tips

1 Hotels
Italian hotels are categorized from 1 (basic) to 5 (deluxe) stars, based largely on the amenities rather than charm or location. At 3 stars and above, all rooms have at least a private bathroom, TV and telephone.

2 Agriturismo (Farm Stays)
Working farms – usually vineyards – can offer accommodation, up to 30 beds. This translates to largely inexpensive lodgings in bucolic settings. Some are luxury, some exceedingly rustic. Local tourist boards have lists of *agriturismi*, as do the three major consortiums Agriturist, Terra Nostra and Turismo Verde.

3 Villa Renting Tips
Ask to see lots of pictures (including from the windows in each direction) and a layout of the property. Find out how many others might share the villa or other houses on the property.

4 Villa Companies
Villa agencies in the UK include Abercrombie & Kent Chapters and Cottages to Castles. In the US, try Rentals in Tuscany, Marjorie Shaw's Insider's Italy, the Parker Company and Villas International.

5 Rooms to Rent
The tourist office has a list of these invariably cheap options, which can range from a lovely room and semi-private access to a cramped spare room in someone's modern apartment. Amount of contact with the family varies, but it can be a great way to meet locals.

6 Camping and Caravanning
Campgrounds *(campeggi)* are widespread, usually on the periphery of towns and on the coast and islands. Italians tend to eschew tents for camper vans. You end up paying almost as much as at a cheap hotel.

7 Hostels
Every city, and a few towns, have cheap beds in sex-segregated, shared dorms. They are full of international students and usually impose a curfew of midnight or so. Most official IYH hostels are on the edges of towns.

8 Should You Reserve?
The best-known hotels can book up months in advance. Florence tends to be overbooked at Easter, and in May and June. Other than that, you should have no problem finding a room.

9 Booking Services
Sometimes for a small fee, tourist offices and private hotel consortiums will help you find a room. The latter can be found at Florence's train station, Pisa's tourist office, Siena's Piazza San Domenico bus stop and San Gimignano's Via San Giovanni. The countless Internet booking services have an assorted stable of hotels in their databases.

10 Quirks That Can Affect the Price
Rooms without private bath or a view, or for stays longer than three days are often cheaper. An extra bed is usually 30–35% more. Breakfast may not be included, parking may be extra, and prices on minibar items and phone calls usually exorbitant.

Left **Money change** Left **Internet service** Right **Newsstand**

10 Banking and Communications

1 Exchanging Money

Always change money at a bank for the best rates. Bring your passport as ID. "Cambio" exchange booths are good out of banking hours. Avoid exchanging a traveller's cheque at a shop or hotel; the rate is miserable.

2 ATMs

The fastest, easiest and cheapest way to get local currency is via an ATM *(bancomat)*, drawing money directly from your home acount.

3 Credit Cards

MasterCard and VISA are the most widely accepted cards. American Express is also accepted in many places, with Diner's Club running a distant third. You can get credit card cash advances from ATMs, but this is an expensive option.

4 Traveller's Cheques

While still the safest way to carry money, traveller's cheques are being overtaken by the evolution of easier and cheaper ATMs. A few cheques are good for emergencies, though. Buy them denominated in dollars or euros.

5 Currency

Along with 15 other EU countries, the currency in Italy is the euro, which replaced the lira in January 2002. Euro coins come in 1, 2, 5, 10,
20 and 50 euro cents and €1 and €2. Bills come in €5, €10, €20, €50, €100, €200 and €500.

6 Public Phones

Most pay phones in Italy now accept only pre-paid phone cards *(scheda telefonica)*. You can buy these in €5 or €10 denominations at tobacconists *(tabacchi)* and newsstands. Some phones still also accept coins. There is also a range of pre-paid *carta telefonica internazionale* which give you a number to call and a code for making international calls.

7 Calling Home

Having loved ones at home call you – say, at your hotel – is invariably cheaper than using the Italian phone system. Otherwise, use the cards described above or international phone booths in major post offices. The cheapest way to call home is with a calling card (with an international plan) tied to your home phone account. To reverse the charges from any phone, dial the international operator on 170. Calls from hotels are usually expensive. If you want to call Italy from abroad, dial your international prefix (011 in the US, 00 in most other countries), then Italy's country code of 39, then the number, including that initial zero (which, in the past, was dropped).

8 Internet Access

Internet rooms and cafés, and pubs with a PC in one corner are popping up constantly (ask at the tourist office; they tend to appear and disappear frequently). Increasingly, hotels are installing a common-use computer with Web access, sometimes free, sometimes for a small fee.

9 Postal Service

Italy's post, while improving, can still be glacially slow. Letters might arrive home in three days or three months. You needn't visit a post office *(ufficio postale)*; just ask any tobacconist or newsagent for stamps *(francobolli)* for the country to which you are mailing; they know the amount to give you. Then drop it in the slot of the post box (usually red) labelled "*per tutte le altre destinazioni*" (not "*per la città*").

10 Receiving Mail

Mail addressed to "[Your Name]/ Fermo Posta/[Town Name], Italia/ITALY" should make it to the main local post office (though it helps to add the postal code, if you can find it). There's a small fee to pick it up, though Amex cardholders can receive for free letters sent to "[Your Name]/Client Mail/ American Express/Via Dante Alghieri 22r/50123 Firenze, Italia/ITALY".

Left **Mail boxes** Left centre *Carabinieri* Right centre **Postcards** Right **Pharmacy**

⑩ Security and Health

1 Emergencies
Dial 113 for general emergencies or the specific number for the police, ambulance or fire brigade *(see box)*. The car breakdown number is a pay towing service.

2 Safety
Italy is a remarkably safe country. Apart from pickpockets, there is little to fear. Violent crime is rare, and though women (especially young foreign women) may be propositioned strenuously, it's mostly harmless. Even so, women should exercise caution when travelling alone. Many Italians drive aggressively, so be careful behind the wheel.

3 Pickpockets
Pickpockets work the crowds on buses and around train stations and other areas where tourists congregate. Keep all your valuables (save a day's-worth of cash) well out of sight.

4 Street Beggars
Beware of forceful beggars including children who may be skilled at lifting valuables in a flash. A common ruse is for a group of children to swarm around the victim holding up pieces of cardboard with words scrawled on them. While you are either trying to fend them off or scrabble around for small change, the pickpocketing has already happened.

5 Scams
Scams, while not particularly rampant, are mostly attempted on the more clueless-seeming tourists. For instance, taxis might try to set the meter for "out of town" rates rather than local, or give the wrong change. Restaurants might try to pad the bill with items not ordered or try and double-charge your credit card.

6 The Police
There are two main police branches you might deal with, the regular *polizia* and the more useful, military-trained, national *carabinieri* force. The police station is called the *questura*.

7 Medical Charges
EU visitors should obtain a European Health Insurance Card (EHIC) from a post office in their home country, which entitles them to emergency medical treatment. Citizens from elsewhere must have medical insurance that covers Italy. Usually you must pay any hospital charges up front and apply for reimbursement. Blue Cross/Blue Shield members can visit affiliated hospitals in Italy.

8 Italian Hospitals
Italian hospitals *(ospedale)* are semi-privatized and efficient. The emergency room is called *pronto soccorso*. For uncomplicated visits not requiring admission, they'll usually give you a check-up and write a prescription with no other paperwork involved. A free medical translating service for tourists is based in Florence *(see box)*.

9 Italian Chemists
Italian pharmacies *(farmacie)* are usually very well equipped and knowledgeable in helping you with minor ailments. At night and on Sundays, a sign is posted at each pharmacy listing which ones in town have the turn to stay open.

10 Food & Water Safety
Italian water is safe to drink everywhere except on trains and any source signposted *"acqua non potabile"*. Food is largely safe, though uncooked seafood is always risky. The BSE scare led to a temporary ban on all beef on the bone. (*Bistecca fiorentina* is made from an inferior cut than the usual T-bone.)

Directory

Medical Translating Service
055 425 0126

Emergency Numbers
112 (carabinieri)
113 (general)
115 (fire)
116 (car breakdown)
118 (ambulance)

Blue Cross/Blue Shield
www.bluecross.com

Left **View of Siena** Right **Villa San Michele, Fiesole**

TOP 10 Historic Hotels

1 Certosa di Maggiano, Siena

Small-scale, luxury hotel converted from a 14th-century monastery. The hotel's best antiques are in the public areas, leaving rooms simple but well-appointed. There's a small pool in the garden. ✪ *Via Certosa 82 • Map E4 • 0577 288 180 • www.certosadimaggiano.it • €€€€€*

2 Loggiato dei Serviti, Florence

High Renaissance-styled rooms in a 1527 building designed by Antonio Sangallo the Elder. The best, if slightly noisier, rooms open onto a magnificent loggia overlooking the square. Canopy beds add to the antique air. ✪ *Piazza Santissima Annunziata 3 • Map P2 • 055 289 592 • www.loggiatodeiservitihotel.it • €€€€*

3 Della Fortezza, Sorano

In 1998, as part of the restoration work, this 16-room hotel was installed in a wing of Sorano's 13th-century castle. Rooms come with wooden ceilings, fantastic countryside views and 19th-century furnishings. And with the high breezes, there is little need of air-conditioning. Closed January and February. ✪ *Piazza Cairoli 5 • Map F5 • 0564 632 010 • www.sovanahotel.it • €€€ • No A/C*

4 Morandi alla Crocetta, Florence

Built as a convent in 1511, the Morandi is owned by an Irishwoman. Some of the beams, antiques and artwork are reproductions, but the frescoes are genuine 16th-century paintings. There are just 10 rooms. ✪ *Via Laura 50 • Map P2 • 055 234 4747 • www.hotelmorandi.it • €€€€*

5 Villa Belvedere, Colle di Val d'Elsa

This was a residence in the 19th century of Tuscany's Lorraine Grand Dukes. The rooms, a mix of old and modern decor, overlook the villa's verdant park with pool and tennis court. ✪ *Via Senese Belvedere, Loc. Belvedere • Map E3/4 • 0577 920 966 • www.villabelvedere.com • €€€ • No A/C*

6 Villa Pitiana, Florence

This much-altered former monastery has hosted the likes of Galileo and Petrarch. It has an outdoor pool and decent restaurant, all immersed in a park on the outskirts of Florence. ✪ *Via Provinciale per Tosi 7 • Map E3 • 055 860 259 • www.villapitiana.com • €€€€ • No A/C*

7 L'Antico Pozzo, San Gimignano

Though predominantly 15th century, bits of the palazzo date back to times when it hosted, variously, Dante and Inquisition trials. Large rooms and iron bedframes lend an antique air, and "superior" rooms come with 17th-century frescoes. ✪ *Via San Matteo 87 • Map D3 • 0577 942 014 • www.anticopozzo.com • €€€*

8 Royal Victoria, Pisa

Pisa's oldest hotel (opened 1839) has had Ruskin and Roosevelt as guests. A few rooms occupy the 10th-century tower base, while some of the Arno-side doubles can be linked to form family suites. ✪ *Lungarno Pacinotti 12 • Map C3 • 050 940 111 • www.royalvictoria.it • €€€ • 40 of 48 rooms with bathroom • private garage*

9 Palazzo Ravizza, Siena

A family-run 17th-century hotel. Some rooms retain their frescoes, and those at the back are quiet and offer views over the hotel's garden. ✪ *Pian de Mantellini 34 • Map E4 • 0577 280 462 • www.palazzoravizza.it • €€€€*

10 Albergo Pietrasanta, Pietrasanta

In 1997 this 17th-century palazzo was opened as an exclusive hotel, with baths sheathed in the marbles of this mining town between Forte dei Marmi and Viareggio. ✪ *Via Garibaldi 35 • Map C2 • 0584 793 726 • www.albergopietrasanta.com • €€€€€*

Price Categories

For a standard,	€	under €50
double room per	€€	€50–€100
night (with breakfast	€€€	€100–€150
if included), taxes	€€€€	€150–€200
and extra charges.	€€€€€	over €200

Left **Helvetia e Bristol, Florence** Right **Waterfront houses, Portoferraio, Elba**

🔟 Luxury Inns

1 Westin Excelsior, Florence

The top address in town, a bastion of luxury and refinement on the Arno. The room furnishings are opulent and there are few amenities the hotel lacks or services it cannot provide. Try for an Arno-side room. ✆ *Piazza Ognisanti 3 • Map K3 • 055 27 151 • www.westin.com • €€€€€*

2 Villa San Michele, Fiesole

Michelangelo is said to have designed the façade on this monastery between Florence and Fiesole. Only doubles inhabit the original building, with the sumptuous suites hiding in half-buried wings overlooking the terraced gardens and pool. ✆ *Via Doccia 4 • Map E2 • 055 567 8200 • www.villasanmichele.com • €€€€€*

3 Helvetia e Bristol, Florence

Though lacking the full suite of amenities at the Excelsior and the fine setting of the San Michele, the Helvetia still feels posher than either. Also, it is the most central of Florence's luxury inns. ✆ *Via de Pescioni 2 • Map M3 • 055 26651 • www.royaldemeure.com • €€€€€*

4 Villa Scacciapensieri

Just outside Siena in hilly parkland and located in a 19th-century villa overlooking the city walls, this hotel has spacious rooms, including three luxury suites. Meals are served on the terraces. There is also a pool and tennis courts. ✆ *Via Scacciapensieri 10 • Map E4 • 0577 41441 • www.villascacciapensieri.it • €€€€*

5 Grand Hotel e La Pace, Montecatini

To most aficionados, the only place to stay in Montecatini. A truly grand villa, set amid five acres of wooded grounds in the centre of town. It sports a frescoed restaurant, pool and exercise room, and spacious rooms. ✆ *Via della Torretta 1 • Map D2 • 0572 75801 • www.grandhotellapace.it • €€€€€*

6 Il Pellicano, Monte Argentario

An oasis of luxury built in 1964 on a particularly wild and scenic bit of coast. Accommodation consists of cottages scattered through the pine, cypress and olive woods, and amenities include a piano bar, gym, beauty spa, tennis courts, seawater pool and waterskiing. ✆ *Loc. Lo Sparcatello • Map E6 • 0564 858 111 • www.pellicanohotel.com • €€€€€*

7 Il Chiostro di Pienza, Pienza

A converted 15th-century convent in the centre of town, with well-appointed and modishly furnished rooms enlarged from monks' cells. Views are over the rolling Val d'Orcia hills. ✆ *Corso Rossellino 26 • Map F4 • 0578 748 400 • www.relaisilchiostrodipienza.com • €€€€*

8 Gallia Palace, Punta Ala

The top hotel in Tuscany's most exclusive coastal resort. It has large, tasteful rooms, a private beach with boats and canoes, beauty spa, swimming pool in the park, weekend candlelit dinners on the lawn and access to a neighbouring golf course. ✆ *Punta Ala • Map D5 • 0564 922 022 • www.galliapalace.it • €€€€€*

9 Villa Ottone, Elba

The classiest place to stay on Elba, especially if you have a room in the original 19th-century villa. But even the 1970s main building has plenty of terraces with sea views. There's also a small pool, tennis court and water sports equipment. ✆ *Loc. Ottone • Map C5 • 0565 933 042 • www.villaottone.com • €€€€–€€€€€*

10 Locanda L'Elisa, Lucca

This 19th-century villa to the south of town has been turned into 10 sumptuously appointed suites surrounded by lush gardens which hide a small pool. ✆ *Via Mora per Pisa 1952 • Map C2 • 0583 379 737 • www.locandalelisa.it • €€€€€*

 Note: *Unless otherwise stated, all hotels accept credit cards, have en-suite bathrooms and air conditioning*

Left **Hotel rating sign** Centre **View over Montepulciano**

TOP 10 Comfortable Inns

1 Hotel San Michele, Cortona
A 15th-century palazzo of High Renaissance architectural panache (creamy plaster against soft grey stone). Beamed ceilings, antiques, rural vistas from many rooms, and yet sited right in the centre of town. ◎ Via Guelfa 15 • Map F4 • 0575 604 348 • www.hotelsan michele.net • €€€

2 Pensione Pendini, Florence
Little has changed in this pensione for over 120 years, save the addition of firm beds and new furnishings. The larger rooms overlooking café-lined Piazza della Repubblica are best. The Abbolafaio brothers' welcome is warm, and they have two other hotels in town (one near the station, the other on the Arno), so are likely to have room. ◎ Via Strozzi 1 • Map M3 • 055 211 170 • www.florenceitaly.net • €€€

3 La Luna, Lucca
A family-run hotel on a quiet cul-de-sac off Lucca's main shopping street. The rooms are split between two buildings; most furnishings are modern, but try for the second floor rooms in the older half, which retain some rich 17th-century frescoes. ◎ Corte Compagni 12 • Map C2 • 0583 493 634 • www. hotellaluna.com • €€

4 Dei Capitani, Montalcino
This was once a barracks for the Sienese army in their last stand against Florentine forces. Now its rustic rooms have serenity and comfort, with sweeping valley views from one side and lofted mini-apartments on the street side. There's also a small pool on the terrace. ◎ La Lapini 6 • Map E4 • 0577 847 227 • www. deicapitani.it • €€€

5 Albergo Scilla, Sovana
In the centre of this quaint town, eight modestly-sized rooms mix the contemporary and the antique – engraved headboards, wooden dressers and exposed walls vie with modern baths and glass table tops. ◎ Via R. Siviero 1–3 • Map F6 • 0564 616 531 • www.sovanahotel.it • €€

6 Flora, Prato
The owners of this centrally located inn live on the top floor, but graciously share their roof terrace with guests, who can enjoy vegetarian meals along with views of the Castello and Palazzo Comunale. ◎ Via Cairoli 31 • Map D/E2 • 0574 33 521 • www.prathotels.it • €€–€€€

7 Il Sole, Massa Marittima
The only hotel within Massa's walls is just 12 years old. A comfortable inn of Liberty-style furnishings and elegant touches such as Persian carpets in the halls. ◎ Corso della Libertà 43 • Map D4/5 • 0566 901 971 • www.ilsolehotel.it • €€

8 Albergo Duomo, Montepulciano
Just steps from Piazza Grande and the cathedral, the family-run Duomo adds rustic accents such as wooden dressers and cast-iron bedsteads to its otherwise comfortably modern decor. There's a small courtyard for al fresco breakfasts in summer. ◎ Via San Donato 14 • Map F4 • 0578 757 473 • www. montelpulcianohotels.it/ duomo • €€ • No A/C

9 Patria, Pistoia
Pistoia has a dearth of decent hotels, but this modern place with many amenities is a good start. It's got a great location, too, halfway between the train station and the Duomo. ◎ Via F. Crispi 8 • Map D2 • 0573 25 187 • www.patriahotel.com • €€

10 Cavaliere Palace, Arezzo
The cream of Arezzo's sorry hotel crop, overhauled twice (in 1995 and 1999) to provide all the amenities in modern, comfortable rooms. It's pretty central, and there's a terrace for breakfasts. ◎ Via Madonna del Prato 83 • Map F3 • 0575 26 836 • www. cavalierehotels.com • €€€

Note: Unless otherwise stated, all hotels accept credit cards, have en-suite bathrooms and air conditioning

Left **View of the island of Elba**

Price Categories

For a standard,	€ under €50
double room per	€€ €50–€100
night (with breakfast	€€€ €100–€150
if included), taxes	€€€€ €150–€200
and extra charges.	€€€€€ over €200

🔟 Budget Gems

1 Pensione Maria Luisa de' Medici, Florence

Wonderfully old-fashioned, its huge rooms stuffed with a mix of antiques and classic 1950s and 60s furnishings. Run by a Welsh ex-pat. ◈ *Via del Corso 1 • Map N3 • 055 280 048 • €€ • 2 of 9 with bath • No A/C • No credit cards • No phone*

2 Piccolo Hotel Puccini, Lucca

Paolo is the friendliest hotelier in town, keeping his little jewel of an inn shipshape. All but two of the smallish but nicely furnished rooms are on the front, and if you lean out you can see the Romanesque façade of San Michele. ◈ *Via di Poggio 9 • Map C2 • 0583 55 421 • www.hotelpuccini. com • €€*

3 Piccolo Hotel Etruria, Siena

In a centre plagued by either overpriced or grotty hotels, tiny Etruria stands proud. Its immaculate rooms with contemporary decor are great value, and the only drawback is the 12:30am curfew. Book early; there are only 13 rooms. ◈ *Via Donzelle 3 • Map E4 • 0577 288 088 • www.hoteletruria.com • €€ • No A/C*

4 Bellavista, Elba

Everything an island retreat should be. The terraces of most rooms enjoy expansive views over the owner's vines and olives to the wooded headland of Sant'Andrea. You can walk these paths to the resort's beach or to a secluded cove. Rooms are simply furnished, tile-floored and comfortable. ◈ *Loc. Sant'Andrea • Map C5 • 0565 908 015 • www.hotel-bellavista.it • €€ • No A/C*

5 Bernini, Siena

Tiny, much-requested hotel in Mauro and Nadia's own home (Mauro may even entertain you with his accordion). Perched atop St Catharine's convent, the whitewashed rooms are quiet, and two have views of the Duomo. ◈ *Via della Sapienza 15 • Map E4 • 0577 289 047 • www.albergobernini.com • €€ • No credit cards • A/C in 2 rooms • 4 of 9 with bath*

6 Il Colombaio, Castellina in Chianti

This converted farmhouse has kept a strong country air, with rustic antiques and bucolic vistas. Commodious rooms open off cosy lounges. There's also a small pool. ◈ *Via Chiantigiana 29 • Map E3 • 0577 740 444 • www. albergoilcolombaio.it • €€€ • No A/C*

7 Il Borghetto, Montepulciano

Another great family-run place, tucked on a side street off the town's main drag. Rooms are cosy, many with rural views and creaky antique furnishings. As an added attraction, a stretch of medieval town wall passes through the property. ◈ *Borgo Buio 7 • Map F4 • 0578 757 535 • www. ilborghetto.it • €€€*

8 Hotel Abaco, Florence

This is a gem of a budget hotel located between the cathedral and the station in a 16th-century building furnished in the Baroque style. Not all rooms have a bathroom. ◈ *Via dei Banchi 1 • Map L3 • 055 230 1919 • www.hotelabaco.it • €€ • 8 rooms not all with bathroom*

9 Etruria, Volterra

Labyrinthine old budget hotel in an 18th-century palazzo. The comforts are basic, but it's well-maintained and friendly. The rooftop gardens have a gate with direct access to the city's pretty public park. ◈ *Via Matteotti 32 • Map D4 • 0588 87 377 • €€ • 21 rooms all with bathroom • No A/C*

10 Italia, Cortona

Just a few steps off the main piazza, the Italia offers standard comforts and modern furnishings; a few rooms even come with views of the country-side, beyond Cortona's rooftops. ◈ *Via Ghibellina 5/7 • Map F4 • 0575 630 254 • www.planhotel.com • €€*

Left **Villa Vignamaggio** Centre **Agriturismo sign** Right **Verrazzano**

⑩ Agriturismo

1 Villa Vignamaggio, Greve in Chianti

This villa (where Mona Lisa was born, *see p34, 61*) and its surrounding cottages form the most sumptuous *agriturismo* in Tuscany. The rooms are painted in strong colours, and the gardens were featured in the film *Much Ado About Nothing*. Tennis courts and two pools round it out. The apartments have A/C, Jacuzzi tubs and cooking facilities. Minimum two nights. ◈ *Villa Vignamaggio • Map E3 • 055 854 661 • www.vigna maggio.it • €€€€–€€€€€*

2 Podere Terreno, Radda in Chianti

Native Roberto and his wife Silvie are your hosts at this old countryside smallholding of seven rustic rooms. Unlike most *agriturismi*, you dine with the hosts and other guests at a long table. ◈ *Strada per Volpaia • Map E3 • 0577 738 312 • www.podereterreno.it • €€€€*

3 Grazia, Orbetello

An 18th-century villa surrounded by apartments sleeping 2–4 people. Guided horse rides are available and the nature reserves are close by. There's also a pool and tennis courts. Three nights minimum. ◈ *Loc. Provincaccia 110 • Map E6 • 0564 881 182 • www. agriturismograzia.com • €€€ • No A/C • No credit cards*

4 I Bonsi, Reggello

A tree-lined avenue leads to this magnificent country residence, which was once a convent, set in parkland overlooking the Arno valley. There are six apartments to let (minimum of three nights). ◈ *Via I Bonsi 47, Località Sant'Agata • Map E3 • 055 284 615 • www.agriturismoibonsi.it • €€€€€ • No A/C*

5 Il Cicalino, Massa Marittima

A complex of converted buildings in a farm/park. Twelve doubles and nine triples, a Tuscan restaurant, pool, football pitch and gym. Mountain bike rental is also available. Minimum stay: three nights. ◈ *Loc. Cicalino • Map D4/5 • 0566 902 031 • www.ilcicalino.it • €–€€€ • No A/C • No phone*

6 Tenuta Castello il Corno, San Casciano

Fourteen apartments, sleeping 2–7, in former peasant quarters around a fine vineyard villa. You can also learn Tuscan cooking. Minimum stay: three nights. ◈ *Malafrasca 64 • Map E3 • 055 824 851 • www.tenutailcorno.com • €–€€€€ • Closed Jan–Feb • No A/C*

7 Fattoria Castello di Pratelli, Incisa

A turretted fortress from the Dark Ages anchors this wine and olive oil estate, where the eight apartments are spacious. There's also a pool and mountain bikes for hire. No minimum stay. ◈ *Via di Pratelli 1A • Map E3 • 055 833 5986 • www. castellodipratelli.it • €–€€ • Closed mid-Nov–mid-Dec • No A/C • No phone*

8 Fattoria Castello di Verrazzano, Greve in Chianti

A 12th-century castle and wine estate that rents six rooms (min 3 nights) and 2 apartments (weekly) in its complex of medieval buildings. Activities tend towards cantina visits and wine tastings, and the restaurant is good. ◈ *Loc. Greti • Map E3 • 055 854 243 • www.verrazzano.com • €€€ • Closed Jan–Feb • No A/C • No phone*

9 Fattoria Maionchi, Lucca

The four large, multi-level apartments, sleeping 4–6, are country-styled. Pretty gardens. ◈ *Loc. Tofori • Map C2 • 0583 978 194 • www.fattoriamaionchi.it • €€€ • No phone*

10 Fattoria di Solaio, Radicóndoli

Fewer amenities but bags of style in this Renaissance villa. Six doubles and three triples (plus larger apartments available Apr–Sep). Three-night minimum in rooms; one week in apartments. ◈ *Loc. Solaio • Map D4 • 0577 791 029 • www.fattoriasolaio.it • €€ • No A/C • No credit cards*

Note: Unless otherwise stated, all properties accept credit cards, have en-suite bathrooms and air conditioning

Villa La Massa

Price Categories

For a standard,	**€**	under €50
double room per	**€€**	€50–€100
night (with breakfast	**€€€**	€100–€150
if included), taxes	**€€€€**	€150–€200
and extra charges.	**€€€€€**	over €200

🔟 Countryside Hotel Retreats

1 Locanda dell'Amorosa, Sinalunga

The "Lover's Inn" moniker dates back to the hotel's 14th-century origins. The large, apartment-like accommodation has a refined rustic style under the more formal brick loggias surrounding the courtyard. ◎ *Loc. L'Amorosa, Sinalunga • Map F4 • 0577 677 211 • www.amorosa.it • €€€€€*

2 Castello Ripa d'Orcia, San Quirico d'Orcia

A fairy-tale hotel, hewn from a 13th-century castle and outbuildings immersed in the green hills of a nature reserve. Relaxation is the order of your stay, with an absence of TVs and telephones in the huge, country-styled rooms and apartments. ◎ *Loc. Ripa d'Orcia • Map F4 • 0577 897 376 • www.castelloripa dorcia.com • €€–€€€*

3 Relais San Pietro, Castiglion Fiorentino

This is a delightful 17th-century farmhouse situated in an idyllic location overlooking a valley. Accommodation is either in the main building or a converted priest's house. Typically Tuscan décor. Dinner is often served on the terrace in summer. ◎ *Loc. Polvano 3 • Map F4 • 0575 650 100 • www. polvano.com • €€€€*

4 Castello di Gargonza, Monte San Savino

Medieval castle turned spectacular hostelry. Though far from civilization, with a fine restaurant and pool, it feels less removed than many a rural retreat. Apartments are also available. ◎ *Loc. Gargonza • Map F4 • 0575 847 021 • www.gargonza.it • €€€*

5 Villa Rosa in Boscorotondo, Panzano

Isolated villa on a thickly forested stretch of Chianti roadside. Spacious rooms feature beamed ceilings and (for those on the front) access on to two large terraces. There's a pool, trails through the woods and excellent set dinners on the terrace in summer. ◎ *Via San Leolino 59 • Map E3 • 055 852 577 • www.resortvillarosa.it • €€–€€€*

6 Castello di Spaltenna, Gaiole

Around the core of a 12th-century castle, this is the Chianti's most luxurious inn. It sports a room for wine tasting, an outdoor pool and a plethora of antiques. Corner rooms, with their lattice of ceiling beams, are best. ◎ *Castello di Spaltenna • Map E3 • 0577 749 483 • www. spaltenna.com • €€€€€*

7 Tenuta di Ricavo, Castellina

A medieval hamlet rebuilt after World War II. Now a select few can rent its 23 perfectly rusticated rooms and suites installed throughout the village. Guests gather around a fire in winter or the pool in summer. ◎ *Loc. Ricavo, 4 • Map E3 • 0577 740 221 • www.ricavo.com • €€€€€*

8 Villa La Massa, Candeli

This Renaissance villa just 7km (4 miles) south of Florence became a hotel in 1953, since when everyone from Churchill to Madonna has lodged here. Tennis courts, a pool and a Tuscan restaurant overlooking the Arno justify its celebration. Closed 15 Nov–Mar. ◎ *Via della Massa 24 • Map E3 • 055 62611 • www.villa lamassa.com • €€€€–€€€€€*

9 Villa La Principessa, near Lucca

This was once the court of the Duke of Lucca. The rooms are large and comfortable, and there is a swimming pool and garden. ◎ *Loc Massa Pisana • Via Nuova per Pisa 1616 • Map C2 • 0583 370 037 • www.hotelprincipessa. com • €€€€€*

10 La Fattoria, Chiusi

An 1850s farmhouse outside Chiusi overlooking the small lake, with eight large country-styled guest rooms. It has a great Tuscan restaurant. ◎ *Via Lago di Chiusi • Map F4/5 • 0578 21 407 • www.la-fattoria.it • €€€*

Left **View over Fiesole** Right **View over Florence**

TOP 10 Hotels with a View

1 Torre di Bellosguardo, Florence

The views from Fiesole are famous, but the panorama from the Bellosguardo hill above the Oltrarno is better, a close-up sweep of the Florence skyline from the gardens and pool of an evocatively medieval retreat. The central tower contains a suite featuring unsurpassed views in four directions. 🛇 *Via Roti Michelozzi 2, Florence* • *Map E3* • *055 229 8145* • *www.torrebellosguardo.com* • *€€€€€* • *A/C in 3 suites*

2 Duomo, Siena

The palazzo is 12th-century, but the rooms (some medium-sized, others cramped) are modern and comfy. The 12 "panoramic" rooms feature Duomo views, including a small top-floor double with windows on three sides and sweeping vistas. 🛇 *Via Stalloreggi 38* • *Map E4* • *0577 289 088* • *www.hotelduomo.it* • *€€€*

3 Villa Kinzica, Pisa

Though the hotel is nothing special, if you get a room on the front or left side you will open your shutters on to a postcard view of the Leaning Tower, a mere stone's throw away. Only half the rooms have A/C, however. 🛇 *Piazza Arcivescovado 2* • *Map C3* • *050 560 419* • *www.hotelvillakinzica.it* • *€€*

4 Chiari Bigallo, Florence

Now being refurbished to three-star status, the Bigallo has long been famous among the Florence budget-conscious for its views of the Duomo group. The only drawback is the noise of pedestrians on the streets below. 🛇 *Via degli Adimari 2* • *055 216 086* • *www.hoteldelanzi.it* • *€€€€*

5 La Cisterna, San Gimignano

Pick your view at this hotel – a cinematographers' favourite (it appeared in *Tea with Mussolini* and *Where Angels Fear to Tread*). Rooms at the front open onto a piazza that supports San Gimignano's famous towers. Those at the back drink in a view of vineyards and hills. 🛇 *Piazza della Cisterna* • *Map D3* • *0577 940 328* • *www.hotelcisterna.it* • *€€€* • *bar & restaurant*

6 Torre Guelfa, Florence

While most rooms in this converted 1280 palazzo don't have great views, the lofty terrace bar has an unbeatable panorama across Florence. 🛇 *Borgo S.S. Apostoli 8* • *Map M4* • *055 239 6338* • *www.hoteltorreguelfa.com* • *€€€€*

7 Il Giglio, Montalcino

Only the eight rooms at the back enjoy the best view in town: cliff-hugging houses to one side and a slope down to Tuscany's countryside to the other. This hotel adds a touch of class to the rusticity. 🛇 *Via Soccorso Saloni 5* • *Map E4* • *0577 846 577* • *www.gigliohotel.com* • *€€*

8 Montorio, Montepulciano

A small hilltop hotel of comfy mini-apartments. The garden has the best views of Renaissance masterpiece Tempio di San Biagio; all rooms have rural vistas. 🛇 *Strada per Pienza 2* • *Map F4* • *0578 717 442* • *www.montorio. com* • *Closed mid-Dec–Feb* • *€€€€*

9 Augustus Lido, Forte dei Marmi

The best of both worlds: a gorgeous beach-side villa, plus access, via an under-the-road tunnel, to the modern hotel Augustus, with its pool, restaurant and live music club. 🛇 *Viale Morin 169* • *Map C2* • *0584 787 200* • *www. versilia.toscana.it/augustus* • *Closed Nov–Mar* • *€€€€€*

10 Gran Duca, Livorno

The only decent lodging in Livorno is right on the harbourfront, and its best rooms overlook Pietro Tacca's *Monument of the Four Moors* and the busy port beyond. Guest rooms are well-appointed, if uninspired, and there's a small fitness centre and spa. 🛇 *Piazza Giuseppe Micheli 16* • *Map C3* • *0586 891 024* • *www.granduca.it* • *€€€*

Note: *Unless otherwise stated, all hotels accept credit cards, have en-suite bathrooms and air conditioning*

Price Categories

For a standard, double room per night (with breakfast if included), taxes and extra charges.

€ under €50
€€ €50–€100
€€€ €100–€150
€€€€ €150–€200
€€€€€ over €200

Left **Montalcino** Right **Montepulciano old town**

🔟 Monasteries & Youth Hostels

1 Ostello Villa Camerata, Florence

Though a 20-minute ride from the centre (bus 17B), you can't get lodging in a 16th-century villa any cheaper. Mostly dorms, though 2- and 3-person family rooms are available. The wooded grounds host a campground. 🅢 *Viale Augusto Righi 2/4 • Map E3 • 055 601 451 • www. ostellionline.com • € • No A/C • No phone*

2 Ostello Archi Rossi, Florence

Arrive early in the day at this popular, well-located hostel that accepts no advance bookings. The hostel also offers laundry facilities, a restaurant and internet access. 🅢 *Via Faenza 94r • Map M2 • 055 290 804 • www.hostelarchirossi.com • € • No A/C • No credit cards • Payphones*

3 Ostello Apuano, Marina di Massa

Set in a coastal park, this villa-hostel offers bike rentals, a beach and plenty of park to enjoy. 11:30pm curfew. Open 16 Mar–Sep; family rooms not available Jul–Aug. 🅢 *Viale delle Pinete, Partaccia 237 • Map C2 • 0585 780 034 • ostelloapuano@hotmail.com • € • No A/C • No credit cards • No phone*

4 Santuario San Caterina/Alma Domus, Siena

The nuns of St Catharine run this simple but comfortable inn. Many rooms have great views across a narrow valley to the striped Duomo. All of the rooms have phones (receiving incoming calls only) and air-conditioning. There's a TV lounge and pay phones in the common rooms. 🅢 *Via Camporeggio 37 • Map E4 • 0577 44 177 • www. hotelalmadomus.it • €€ • No credit cards*

5 Villa I Cancelli, Florence

A 15th-century palazzo in the hills above Florence, a 15-minute drive from the centre. There are rural views from the 31 simple bedrooms. The gates shut at 11pm, though the sisters will reopen them to let you back in later if need be. 🅢 *Via Incontri 21 • Map E2 • 055 422 6001 • €€ • No A/C • No credit cards • No phone*

6 Ostello San Marco, Cortona

Located in an old convent, this hostel has 80 beds in rooms for two, four, six or eight people. The management arranges visits to local Etruscan sites. Midnight curfew. 🅢 *Via Maffei 57 • Map F4 • 0575 601 765 • www.cortonahostel.com • € • No A/C • No credit cards • No phone*

7 Ostello del Chianti, Tavernelle Val di Pesa

Activies here are geared toward wine production and tasting. It has some family rooms. Break-feasts and packed lunches are available for an extra cost. SITA buses stop nearby. Closed Nov–14 March. 🅢 *Via Roma 137 • Map E3 • 055 805 0265 • € • No A/C • No credit cards • No phone*

8 Ostello San Frediano, Lucca

Outside the town walls (take buses 59, 60, 3 or navetta 2). A mix of dorms and family rooms, some with private bathroom. 🅢 *Via della Cavallerizza 12 • Map C2 • 0583 469 957 • www.ostellolucca.it • € • No A/C • No credit cards • No phone*

9 Monastero di Camáldoli

The Benedictine Rule forbids turning away travellers, and so drop-in guests as well as those signed up to the week-long workshops (Easter–mid-Sep) are welcomed. 🅢 *Loc. Camáldoli • Map F2 • 0575 556 012 • www. camaldoli.it • € • No A/C • No credit cards • No phone*

10 Monte Oliveto Maggiore

A gorgeously frescoed monastery in the hills, offering single and double rooms with private baths (Easter–Oct), and selling honey, herbs and wines. 🅢 *Abbazia di Monte Oliveto Maggiore • Map E4 • 0577 707 652 • www. monteolivetomaggiore.it • € • No A/C • No credit cards • No phone*

Index

Page numbers in **bold** type refer to main entries.

Index

Acknowledgements

The Author

Reid Bramblett is a travel writer who lives outside Philadelphia, USA. As well as this book, he has also written guides to Italy, Europe and New York for Frommer's and the *For Dummies* series.

Produced by Blue Island Publishing, Highbury, London

Editorial Director Rosalyn Thiro
Art Director Stephen Bere
Editors Michael Ellis, Charlotte Rundall
Designers Tony Foo, Ian Midson
Picture Research Ellen Root
Research Assistance Amia Allende, Emma Wilson
Proofreader Stewart J. Wild
Index Hilary Bird
Fact Checker Matt Finley
Additional Contributions Alexandra Lawrence

Main Photographer Linda Whitwam

Additional Photography
Philip Enticknap, Kim Gamble, Steve Gorton, John Heseltine, Kim Sayer, Clive Streeter

Artwork Richard Draper, Chris Orr & Associates

Cartography
Encompass Graphics

AT DORLING KINDERSLEY:
Director of Publishing Gillian Allan
Senior Publishing Manager Louise Bostock Lang
Publishing Manager Kate Poole
Senior Editor Marcus Hardy
Senior Art Editor Marisa Renzullo
Cartography Co-ordinator Casper Morris
DTP Jason Little
Production Sarah Dodd, Marie Ingledew
Additional Editorial Assistance Michelle Crane, Conrad van Dyk, Sam Merrell, Rebecca Milner, Rada Radojicic, Ellie Smith

Picture Credits

Dorling Kindersley would like to thank all the cathedrals, churches, museums, hotels, restaurants, shops, galleries, vineyards and other sights for their assistance and kind permission to photograph at their establishments.

Placement Key: t–top; tl–top left; tr–top right; c–centre; cb–centre below; b–bottom; bl–bottom left; br–bottom right; l–left; d–detail

AFE, Rome: Roberto del Mazza 102b; AKG, London: Rabatti-Dominigie (photographer), Palazzo Pitti, Florence, Titian's *The Penitent Mary Magdalene* 16br.

BRIDGEMAN ART LIBRARY, London: Baptistry, Florence, Lorenzo Ghiberti's *The Gates of Paradise* 12–13; Bargello, Florence, Donatello's *David* (c.1440) 48b; Giambologna's *Mercury* (1589) 51l; Biblioteca Reale, Turin, Leonardo da Vinci's *Portrait of Bearded Man* (possibly a self portrait, c.1513) 50c; Uffizi, Florence, Sandro Botticelli's *Adoration of the Magi* 11t, *The Birth of Venus* 8bl(d), 52b, *Primavera* (c.1478) 9t; Michelangelo's *Holy Family with St John (Doni Tondo)* 6tr, 8br; Fra Filippo Lippi's *Madonna and Child with Angels* (c.1455) 10b; Raphael's *Madonna del Cardellino* 10tr, *Portraits of Leo X, Cardinal Luigi de'Rossi and Giulo de Medici* (1518) 54b, *Self Portrait* 50tr(d); Titian's *Venus of Urbino* 9b; Giorgio Vasari's *Lorenzo the Magnificent* 54c; Leonardo da Vinci's *The Annunciation* (1472–5; post-restoration) 8tr(d), 10tl(d); Museo Civico, Prato, panel from Bernardo Daddi's *The Legend of the Sacred Girdle* 29b, 93t(d); Museo dell'Opera del Duomo, Florence,

Acknowledgements

Michelangelo's *Pietà* (1553) 13b;
Museo Diocesano, Cortona, Fra
Angelico's *The Annunciation* 38–9;
Museo di Firenze Com'era,
Florence, Giusto Utens' *Villa
Poggio a Caiano* (1599) 60b;
Museo di San Marco dell'Angelico,
Florence, Fra Angelico's *The
Annunciation* (c.1438–45) 53tl;
Palazzo Pitti, Florence, photograph
of façade designed by Filippo
Brunelleschi 14t, 16tr, 48tr, 49cb(d);
Antonio Canova's *Venus* (1810;
lateral view) 17; Raphael's *The
Madonna of the Chair* 16bl;
photograph of Sala di Marte
(Hall of Mars, 17th century)
6bl,14–15, 16tl; photograph of
Salone di Giovanni da San Giovanni
77t; Pinacoteca, Sansepolcro,
Piero della Francesca's *The
Resurrection* (c.1463) 49tl; San
Michele, Carmignano, Prato,
Jacopo Pontormo's *The Visitation*
51b; Santa Croce, Florence, Giotto
di Bondone's *Death of Saint Francis*
50tl(d); Villa Demidoff, Pratolino,
Giambologna's *The Appennines*
(1580) 60c.

CAFFE LA TORRE: 104tc, 104bl;
LA CANTINETTA DI RIGNANA: 72tl;
JOE CORNISH: 39b, 98–9.

HOTEL HELVETIA & BRISTOL:
143tl.

MARKA, Milano: R. Abbate 66tr,
67; G. Andreini 66c; P. Guerrini 66b;
M. Motta 141tr; F. Tovoli 66tl.

RETROGRAPH ARCHIVE, London:
108tr; RISTORANTE LA MORA:
111tl; RISTORANTE OLTRE IL
GIARDINO: 97tl.

SCALA GROUP, Florence: Medici
Chapel, Florence, Michelangelo's
Tomba di Giuliano duca di Nemours
45c; Camposanto, Pisa, *Ippogrifo*
23t; Uffizi, Florence, Spinario's *Io
Boy Removing Thorn* 11b; Museo
Archeologico, Grosseto, Cratere
di Pescia Romana 41t; Musei
Civici, San Gimignano,
Pinturicchio's *Madonna e i SS.
Gregorio e Benedetto* 18b; Museo
Nazionale di S. Matteo, Simone
Martini's *Polittico* 24c; Palazzo
Pubblico, Siena, Simone Martini's
*Guioriccio da Fogliano all'assedio
di Monte Massi* 30b(d), 32t(d),
Maestà 33b; Tomba del Colle,
Chiusi, *Scene con danzatori e
suonatori* 40t.

All other images are © Dorling
Kindersley. For further information
see www.dkimages.com

Special Editions of DK Travel Guides

DK Travel Guides can be purchased
in bulk quantities at discounted prices
for use in promotions or as premiums.
We are also able to offer special
editions and personalized jackets,
corporate imprints, and excerpts from
all of our books, tailored specifically to
meet your own needs.

To find out more, please contact:
(in the United States)
SpecialSales@dk.com
(in the UK) **TravelSpecialSales@uk.
dk.com**
(in Canada) DK Special Sales at
general@tourmaline.ca
(in Australia) **business.development@
pearson.com.au**

Phrase Book

In an Emergency

Help!	**Aiuto!**	eye-yoo-toh
Stop!	**Fermate!**	fair-mah-teh
Call a doctor.	**Chiama un medico**	kee-ah-mah oon meh-dee-koh
Call an ambulance.	**Chiama un' ambulanza**	kee-ah-mah oon am-boo-lan-tsa
Call the police.	**Chiama la polizia**	kee-ah-mah lah pol-ee-tsee-ah
Call the fire brigade.	**Chiama i pompieri**	kee-ah-mah ee pom-pee-air-ee

Communication Essentials

Yes/No	**Sì/No**	see/noh
Please	**Per favore**	pair fah-vor-eh
Thank you.	**Grazie**	grah-tsee-eh
Excuse me	**Mi scusi**	mee skoo-zee
Hello	**Buon giorno**	bwon jor-noh
Goodbye	**Arrivederci**	ah-ree-veh-dair-chee
Good evening	**Buona sera**	bwon-ah sair-ah
What?	**Quale?**	kwah-leh?
When?	**Quando?**	kwan-doh?
Why?	**Perchè?**	pair-keh?
Where?	**Dove?**	doh-veh?

Useful Phrases

How are you?	**Come sta?**	koh-meh stah?
Very well, thank you.	**Molto bene, grazie.**	moll-toh beh-neh grah-tsee-eh
Pleased to meet you.	**Piacere di conoscerla.**	pee-ah-chair-eh dee-coh-noh-shair-lah
That's fine.	**Va bene.**	va beh-neh
Where is/are…?	**Dov'è/ Dove sono…?**	dov-eh/doveh soh-noh?
How do I get to…?	**Come faccio per arrivare a…?**	koh-meh fah-choh pair arri-var-eh ah…?
Do you speak English?	**Parla inglese?**	par-lah een-gleh-zeh?
I don't understand.	**Non capisco.**	non ka-pee-skoh
I'm sorry.	**Mi dispiace.**	mee dee-spee-ah-cheh

Shopping

How much does this cost?	**Quant'è, per favore?**	kwan-teh pair fah-vor-eh?
I would like…	**Vorrei…**	vor-ray
Do you have…?	**Avete…?**	ah-veh-teh… ?
Do you take credit cards?	**Accettate carte di credito?**	ah-chet-tah-teh kar-teh dee creh-dee-toh?
What time do you open/close?	**A che ora apre/ chiude?**	ah keh or-ah ah-preh/kee-oo-deh?
this one	**questo**	kweh-stoh
that one	**quello**	kwell-oh
expensive	**caro**	kar-oh
cheap	**a buon prezzo**	ah bwon pret-soh
size, clothes	**la taglia**	lah tah-lee-ah
size, shoes	**il numero**	eel noo-mair-oh
white	**bianco**	bee-ang-koh
black	**nero**	neh-roh
red	**rosso**	ross-oh
yellow	**giallo**	jal-loh
green	**verde**	vair-deh
blue	**blu**	bloo

Types of Shop

bakery	**il forno /il panificio**	eel forn-oh /eel pan-ee-fee-choh
bank	**la banca**	lah bang-kah
bookshop	**la libreria**	lah lee-breh-ree-ah
cake shop	**la pasticceria**	lah pas-tee-chair-ee-ah
chemist	**la farmacia**	lah far-mah-chee-ah
delicatessen	**la salumeria**	lah sah-loo-meh-ree-ah
department store	**il grande magazzino**	eel gran-deh mag-gad-zee-noh
grocery	**alimentari**	ah-lee-men-tah-ree
hairdresser	**il parrucchiere**	eel par-oo-kee-air-eh
ice cream parlour	**la gelateria**	lah jel-lah-tair-ree-ah
market	**il mercato**	eel mair-kah-toh
newsstand	**l'edicola**	leh-dee-koh-lah
post office	**l'ufficio postale**	loo-fee-choh pos-tah-leh
supermarket	**il supermercato**	eel su-pair-mair-kah-toh
tobacconist	**il tabaccaio**	eel tah-bak-eye-oh
travel agency	**l'agenzia di viaggi**	lah-jen-tsee-ah dee vee-ad-jee

Sightseeing

art gallery	**la pinacoteca**	lah peena-koh-teh-kah
bus stop	**la fermata dell'autobus**	lah fair-mah-tah dell ow-toh-booss
church	**la chiesa**	lah kee-eh-zah
	la basilica	lah bah-seel-i-kah
closed for holidays	**chiuso per le ferie**	kee-oo-zoh pair leh fair-ee-eh
garden	**il giardino**	eel jar-dee-no
museum	**il museo**	eel moo-zeh-oh
railway station	**la stazione**	lah stah-tsee-oh-neh
tourist information	**l'ufficio di turismo**	loo-fee-choh dee too-ree-smoh

Staying in a Hotel

Do you have any vacant rooms?	**Avete camere libere?**	ah-veh-teh kah-mair-eh lee-bair-eh?
double room	**una camera doppia**	oona kah-mair-ah doh-pee-ah
with double bed	**con letto matrimoniale**	kon let-toh mah-tree-moh-nee-ah-leh
twin room	**una camera con due letti**	oona kah-mair-ah kon doo-eh let-tee
single room	**una camera singola**	oona kah-mair-ah sing-goh-lah
room with a bath, shower	**una camera con bagno, con doccia**	oona kah-mair-ah kon ban-yoh, kon dot-chah
I have a reservation.	**Ho fatto una prenotazione**	oh fat-toh oona preh-noh-tah tsee-oh-neh

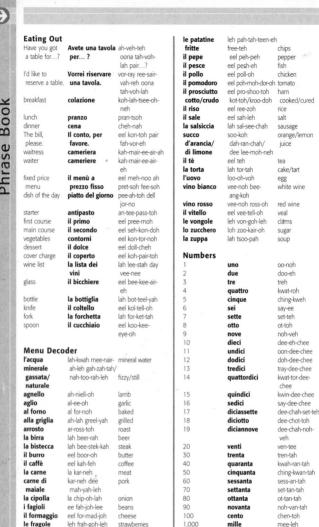

Phrase Book

Eating Out

Have you got a table for…?	**Avete una tavola per… ?**	ah-veh-teh oona tah-voh-lah pair…?
I'd like to reserve a table.	**Vorrei riservare una tavola.**	vor-ray ree-sair-vah-reh oona tah-voh-lah
breakfast	**colazione**	koh-lah-tsee-oh-neh
lunch	**pranzo**	pran-tsoh
dinner	**cena**	cheh-nah
The bill, please.	**Il conto, per favore.**	eel kon-toh pair fah-vor-eh
waitress	**cameriera**	kah-mair-ee-air-ah
waiter	**cameriere**	kah-mair-ee-air-eh
fixed price menu	**il menù a prezzo fisso**	eel meh-noo ah pret-soh fee-soh
dish of the day	**piatto del giorno**	pee-ah-toh dell jor-no
starter	**antipasto**	an-tee-pass-toh
first course	**il primo**	eel pree-moh
main course	**il secondo**	eel seh-kon-doh
vegetables	**contorni**	eel kon-tor-noh
dessert	**il dolce**	eel doll-cheh
cover charge	**il coperto**	eel koh-pair-toh
wine list	**la lista dei vini**	lah lee-stah day vee-nee
glass	**il bicchiere**	eel bee-kee-air-eh
bottle	**la bottiglia**	lah bot-teel-yah
knife	**il coltello**	eel kol-tell-oh
fork	**la forchetta**	lah for-ket-tah
spoon	**il cucchiaio**	eel koo-kee-eye-oh

Menu Decoder

l'acqua minerale gassata/ naturale	lah-kwah mee-nair-ah-leh gah-zah-tah/ nah-too-rah-leh	mineral water fizzy/still
agnello	ah-niell-oh	lamb
aglio	al-ee-oh	garlic
al forno	al for-noh	baked
alla griglia	ah-lah greel-yah	grilled
arrosto	ar-ross-toh	roast
la birra	lah beer-rah	beer
la bistecca	lah bee-stek-kah	steak
il burro	eel boor-oh	butter
il caffè	eel kah-feh	coffee
la carne	la kar-neh	meat
carne di maiale	kar-neh dee mah-yah-leh	pork
la cipolla	la chip-oh-lah	onion
i fagioli	ee fah-joh-lee	beans
il formaggio	eel for-mad-joh	cheese
le fragole	leh frah-goh-leh	strawberries
il fritto misto	eel free-toh mees-toh	mixed fried dish
la frutta	la froot-tah	fruit
frutti di mare	froo-tee dee mah-reh	seafood
i funghi	ee foon-ghee	mushrooms
i gamberi	ee gam-bair-ee	prawns
il gelato	eel jel-lah-toh	ice cream
l'insalata	leen-sah-lah-tah	salad
il latte	eel laht-teh	milk
lesso	less-oh	boiled
il manzo	eel man-tsoh	beef
l'olio	loh-lee-oh	oil
il pane	eel pah-neh	bread
le patate	leh pah-tah-teh	potatoes
le patatine fritte	leh pah-tah-teen-eh free-teh	chips
il pepe	eel peh-peh	pepper
il pesce	eel pesh-eh	fish
il pollo	eel poll-oh	chicken
il pomodoro	eel poh-moh-dor-oh	tomato
il prosciutto cotto/crudo	eel pro-shoo-toh kot-toh/kroo-doh	ham cooked/cured
il riso	eel ree-zoh	rice
il sale	eel sah-leh	salt
la salsiccia	lah sal-see-chah	sausage
succo d'arancia/ di limone	soo-koh dah-ran-chah/ dee lee-moh-neh	orange/lemon juice
il tè	eel teh	tea
la torta	lah tor-tah	cake/tart
l'uovo	loo-oh-voh	egg
vino bianco	vee-noh bee-ang-koh	white wine
vino rosso	vee-noh ross-oh	red wine
il vitello	eel vee-tell-oh	veal
le vongole	leh von-goh-leh	clams
lo zucchero	loh zoo-kair-oh	sugar
la zuppa	lah tsoo-pah	soup

Numbers

1	**uno**	oo-noh
2	**due**	doo-eh
3	**tre**	treh
4	**quattro**	kwat-roh
5	**cinque**	ching-kweh
6	**sei**	say-ee
7	**sette**	set-teh
8	**otto**	ot-toh
9	**nove**	noh-veh
10	**dieci**	dee-eh-chee
11	**undici**	oon-dee-chee
12	**dodici**	doh-dee-chee
13	**tredici**	tray-dee-chee
14	**quattordici**	kwat-tor-dee-chee
15	**quindici**	kwin-dee-chee
16	**sedici**	say-dee-chee
17	**diciassette**	dee-chah-set-teh
18	**diciotto**	dee-chot-toh
19	**diciannove**	dee-chah-noh-veh
20	**venti**	ven-tee
30	**trenta**	tren-tah
40	**quaranta**	kwah-ran-tah
50	**cinquanta**	ching-kwan-tah
60	**sessanta**	sess-an-tah
70	**settanta**	set-tan-tah
80	**ottanta**	ot-tan-tah
90	**novanta**	noh-van-tah
100	**cento**	chen-toh
1,000	**mille**	mee-leh
2,000	**duemila**	doo-eh mee-lah
1,000,000	**un milione**	oon meel-yoh-neh

Time

one minute	**un minuto**	oon mee-noo-toh
one hour	**un'ora**	oon or-ah
a day	**un giorno**	oon jor-noh
Monday	**lunedì**	loo-neh-dee
Tuesday	**martedì**	mar-teh-dee
Wednesday	**mercoledì**	mair-koh-leh-dee
Thursday	**giovedì**	joh-veh-dee
Friday	**venerdì**	ven-air-dee
Saturday	**sabato**	sah-bah-toh
Sunday	**domenica**	doh-meh-nee-kah